The End of the East German Economy

From Honecker to Reunification

Phillip J. Bryson

Professor of Managerial Economics,
Brigham Young University, Provo, Utah

Manfred Melzer

Senior Researcher,
German Institute for Economic Research, Berlin, Germany

St. Martin's Press   New York

First published in the United States of America in 1991

Printed in Hong Kong

ISBN 0-312-05556-0

Library of Congress Cataloging-in-Publication Data
Bryson, Phillip J.
The end of the East German Economy : from Honecker to
reunification / Phillip J. Bryson, Manfred Melzer.
p.   cm.
Includes bibliographical references and index.
ISBN 0-312-05556-0
1. Germany (East)—Economic policy. 2. Germany (East)—Economic
conditions. 3. Central planning—Germany (East). 4. Germany (East)—
Commerce. I. Melzer, Manfred. II. Title.
HC290.78B8   1991
338.943'009'048—dc20   90-45275
                                                            CIP

THE END OF THE EAST GERMAN ECONOMY

To all those East Germans whose courage helped obliterate the Wall and bring socialist economic planning to an end in their country.

Contents

Preface

After the collapse of the Honecker regime, we learned much about the German Democratic Republic (GDR) that we could only suspect before. Even those who had retained a healthy skepticism toward East German socialism had not been suspicious enough. This became apparent when the activities of the party's security arm, the National Security Service (*Staatssicherheitsdienst* or 'Stasi'), were finally exposed to public light. A primary function of that organization was to 'defend' East German economic success through domestic intelligence activities. In reality, the Service created a 'surveillance system of the greatest perfection.'[1] It grew dramatically after 1985 in order to solve political problems generally through the administration of punitive measures.

People unsympathetic to the objectives of the party ('people who think differently' or *Andersdenkende*) were to be sought out and appropriate action was to be taken against them. There could be neither political discussion nor compromise with such individuals. In a society in which emigration was impossible, such action could and did assure a macabre domestic tranquillity. Within certain parameters, the East German government required unfailing control over the actions of its people. At the same time, of course, it felt the necessity to provide them with the basic things competitive societies can provide. When the borders of the German Democratic Republic (GDR) were no longer impenetrable, management of the populace was no longer assured. The economy was so interlaced with systemic problems that the regime's endeavours to provide the good life for

---

[1] See 'Seit 1985 "flaechendeckende" Ueberwachung angestrebt', *National Zeitung*, no. 13, 16 January 1990, p. 4. This East German publication revealed the nature of the organization at the time it was dissolved. See also, *Neue Zeit: Tageszeitung der Christlich-Demokratischen Union Deutschlands*, 16 January 1990, pp. 1, 3. The surveillance system included over a thousand agents responsible for monitoring telephones, which may be suggestive of the number of phones that function at any given time in the GDR. Over 2,000 agents monitored the mails.

the people were beginning to falter. Moreover, the malady of the economic mechanism appeared unresponsive to first aid when the labor haemorrhage could not be stopped.

We will have little to say in this brief volume about the politics of the Honecker era. Reference was made to the National Security Service because that political institution reveals much about why the East German economy functioned reasonably well for a time, but was destined ultimately to fail. Although not generally apparent to the non-specialist, much about the GDR seemed rather liberal for a Marxist-Leninist regime: its openness to information from the West, the relatively progressive travel policy of the past two or three years, the existence of a private sector (the handicrafts) in the economy, and the steadily improving GDR living standards.[2] For those who failed to be sufficiently impressed with the economic achievements, vitally important social peace and a veneer of societal harmony were maintained at least in good part by the activities of the National Security Service.

Other basic GDR political institutions were also of the traditional socialist type. There was no 'new thinking' in the GDR, no permitted deviation from the official line. The expanded travel rights, the increased autonomy granted to the combines after 1980, and other policies of token liberalization had to remain within the narrow parameters laid down by the party. The political environment may have ensured social 'harmony', but over time the oppression created resentments which led to flight as soon as the opportunity revealed itself.

In comparison with other socialist countries in the final phase of Marxism-Leninism, East Germany was apparently the most effective economically. It was a different story, however, when comparisons were made with the economically powerful Federal Republic of Germany (FRG, or West Germany). The larger productivity and living standard gaps between the two Germanies were readily apparent.

In the first half of the 1980s, genuine improvements were visible in the GDR. In the last half of the 1980s, after the party leaders had

---

[2] See Phillip J. Bryson, *The Consumer Under Socialist Planning: The East German Case* (New York: Praeger, 1984).

become very confident of the superiority of their path to socialism, performance began to weaken dramatically. It is doubtful that top East German leaders themselves knew how badly things were going. Plan fulfilment reports can always be embellished, statistics can be managed, and top leaders can be told what they desire to hear.

Nevertheless, because sufficient information was available before 1989 and additional information came to light thereafter, the functioning of the GDR economy under Honecker is certainly not locked in mystery. The amelioration of economic organization and performance of the early 1980s and the decline of the final phase can be documented.

At the fortieth anniversary of the founding of the GDR, just days before the disintegration of the Honecker regime, a featured guest of the celebrations, Mikhail Gorbachev, observed that 'life punishes those who change too late.' As will be apparent in this brief book, especially in Chapter 1, this axiom might be the epitaph of an East German regime guilty of the failings of omission and commission related in this book. There were some high points of achievement in the history of the Honecker regime, but there were also too many occasions in which the desire to maintain absolute power prevented sound economic decisions. Chapter 1 will review the growing external pressure that perestroika created and the fatally insufficient response of the Honecker regime to that pressure.

The economic performance of the East German economy in the final phases of the Honecker era will be investigated in Chapter 2. The historical foundations of that performance, particularly as it affected the domestic economy, will be examined. The international dimensions of the combine planning system will be addressed in Chapter 3. There we will observe how the East German economic system functioned as a part of East Europe's 'socialist economic integration' with other members of the Council for Mutual Economic Assistance (CMEA), which is the Warsaw Pact's economic version of a 'common market.'

Chapter 4 will survey the shortage conditions which characterized the GDR economy after the 'turning point' (or *Wende*) between the Honecker years and new era had been passed. The new era promised initially to be one of economic, political, and social reform, the rough blueprints of which are the topic of Chapter 4. Here we see the public discussion on reform that preceded the interesting but incomplete conceptual design that resulted. That New era was important because it showed the rather hopeless cleft between the aspirations of socialism and reality's harsh constraints on the possibilities for change. In fact, the heralded new era was a mere transition. We review in Chapter 5 the actual reform measures taken and the reform legislation enacted by the interim government. We will show there how the attempts to decentralize and open the economy were submerged with almost unfathomable speed in a more completely transforming process, the tidal wave of German reunification. The result is now history: on 3 October, 1990, the day of German unity, five new East German *Bundesländer* joined the Federal Republic of Germany, or 'Deutschland'.

The authors wish to thank colleagues and staff of their respective institutions, the German Institute of Economic Research in (at that time, West) Berlin and Brigham Young University for support in preparing this book. Professor Bryson expresses gratitude to the International Research and Exchanges Board (IREX), the Ministry for Higher Education of the GDR, and the University of Economic Science, 'Bruno Leuschner' in (what was then, East) Berlin, for making possible a research stay in spring of 1989. Prof. Helmut Richter and Dr Hans-Gerd Bannasch of the university's (former) Institute for Socialist Economic Management contributed immensely to Bryson's research there. The Smith Center for Free Enterprise Studies at Brigham Young University helped fund travel necessary for the final preparation of the manuscript. The authors thank Lisa McKirdy for much appreciated editorial assistance, and Milan Minarchik for preparing the index. We are both grateful to our families for their support in this as in all our professional endeavours.

1 Introduction: Perestroika and the Failures of Honecker

In October of 1989 the era of Erich Honecker, General Secretary of East Germany's communist party, came to a well-deserved end. His retirement 'for health reasons' was announced by the East German politburo. Egon Krenz assumed leadership for what turned out to be a brief interlude, promising that a *Wende* (turning point) had been reached. It was not perfectly clear, however, what that *Wende* might bring in terms of social change and economic policy. The possibilities of the future were bounded, as always, by resource constraints, economic organization, and entrenched socialist institutions.

Having long tracked the developments of central planning in the German Democratic Republic (GDR), the authors intend in this brief work to undertake an evaluation of the Honecker economic legacy and to explore the economic problems that led the new regime at an incredibly early point after the cataclysm to seek reunification with the Federal Republic of Germany. Clearly, the accomplishments and failures of the Honecker years shaped the possibilities and constraints for the GDR's future.

We begin by considering some of the developments of recent years that led to the collapse of the Honecker regime. They occurred in the highly publicized era of glasnost, perestroika, and *demokratizatsiya*, a period in which the East German communist party (Socialist Unity Party, or SED) gained considerable notoriety for its negative stance on economic and social reform. To the SED it was largely irrelevant that Poland and Hungary were irrevocably committed to a reform course, or that the Soviet Union, the most equal of all the socialist brother countries, was itself attempting a 'revolutionary' restructuring of the economy. For the GDR these developments were not sufficient reason to launch its own reforms.

East Germany did not always show great reluctance to introduce substantive changes into its economic system. With the introduction of its 'New Economic System' in 1963 it had been the first of the East European economies to introduce reforms in the decade of the 1960s. One might wonder, therefore, why the leadership of Gorbachev failed to inspire new reform attempts in East Germany. We will see why, considering reform developments in the Soviet Union, the position of Honecker's GDR may have been less unreasonable than seemed apparent at the time. We will also see that the mismanagement of the economy and society had placed Honecker's regime on a collision course with destiny. First, we review briefly the nature of the reforms being attempted under Gorbachev, then consider in some detail how the Honecker leadership responded to the challenge of perestroika.

THE GDR AND THE SOVIET ECONOMIC REFORM MODEL

Gorbachev's pointed criticisms of the inflexible, inefficient, stagnating, and technologically sluggish Soviet economy had become widely known in the Honecker era. So were the dramatic (if not immediately successful) efforts of President Gorbachev to produce change in both economic and political reality. Gorbachev became aware rather early after his ascent to power in the USSR that even radical structural reform could succeed only if what he called the 'human factor' could be effectively addressed. Fundamental changes, including democratization and glasnost, were the General Secretary's response to the 'human factor' problem. They were introduced to try to provide badly needed motivation for workers, managers, and scientists to create and apply innovations, to achieve higher quality industrial outputs, and to increase the disastrously low level of Soviet productivity.

In order to evaluate the East German claim that there was no need for perestroika in the GDR, let us briefly compare some of the principal conceptions of Soviet reform to those of the East German structural reorganization of the early 1980s.[1] Space limitations preclude all but a summary review of the high points, but the key features of perestroika are rather widely known in any case. They include the following key elements:

- private property restrictions persist, but some flexibility is sought through the formation of cooperatives, which are not subject to the same ministerial regulations that curtail the manoeuvrability of state-owned enterprises. The attempt to free private ownership from traditional and ideology strictures continues.

- greater autonomy and responsibility for the enterprise, based on 'full economic accounting' (*khozraschet*). This simply means that the enterprise is to pay its own way and cover its own costs, functioning in a profitable manner. It includes the right of the enterprise to develop its own economic plans, to lay off redundant workers, and to go bankrupt.

- new techniques for price formation with greater reliance on contracts for inter-enterprise transactions.

- expanded worker participation in management selection and in enterprise decision making, with glasnost and democratization intended to encourage worker support of change and general opposition to bureaucratic resistance.

- reduced planning activities for ministries and central authorities, which are to restrict their activities primarily to perspective planning, technology policy, inter-sectoral activities, and so on.

- declining reliance on state orders, which are to be issued only

---

[1] Cf. Phillip J. Bryson, 'Soviet Economic and Social Reform (*Perestroika and Glasnost*): Claim and Reality', *Wirtschaftssysteme im Umbruch: Markt- und Planwirtschaften zwischen Anpassungszwang and nationalem Reformbedarf* (The Transformation of Economic Systems: Market and Planned Economies between the Necessity for International Adaptation and National Reform), ed. Dieter Cassel, (Munich: Vahlen Verlag, 1990), pp. 123–52.

for key industrial products; only planning normatives and other indirect means of control are to be utilized by the planning authorities.

- increased private activity is to result from the legalization of small, family-type handicraft and service enterprises, but 'moonlighting' and many second-economy activities remain illegal.
- leasing of land for private use over long periods of time is pursued as a means of overcoming the stagnation of collectivization and the ownership arrangements that deny private property.

A decade before the *Wende*, the GDR published numerous new laws on combine formation and refinements of their planning regulations. In the course of the intervening period, we have reviewed the implications of combine formation and of the legislative outpouring which complemented organizational change.[2] For the present purposes, we wish merely to cast a brief glance back at the adumbration of a system design of the primary document[3] of combine formation. There are some interesting similarities in the regulatory blueprints of East Germany's 'plan improving' or 'plan perfecting' (*Planvervollkommnung*) and the Soviet Union's perestroika, as well as the expected differences. When one considers both the similarities and dissimilarities, one almost gets the impression that Soviet reality lagged even further behind the perestroika rhetoric than did the GDR economy, which was so strongly criticized for refusing to adopt perestroika.

Beginning with the similarities, one is struck first with the importance (in both East German plan 'perfecting' and Soviet *perestroika*) of efforts to get production units to adopt economic accounting or

---

2 See, as a single example, our 'Planning Refinements and Combine Formation', *The Carl Beck Papers in Russian and East European Studies*, Center for Russian and East European Studies, University of Pittsburgh, March 1987. A number of others are also cited through this book.

3 *Gesetzblatt der Deutschen Demokratischen Republik*, 'Verordnung über die volkseigenen Kombinate, Kombinatsbetriebe und volkseigenen Betriebe', Teil 1 Nr. 38, (13 November 1979) pp. 355–66.

Khozraschet, so that they function responsibly and profitably. GDR legislation[4] insists that all combines will function according to those principles. Worker participation in combine management is also foreseen in the East German scheme, which notes that the combine's DG (Director General) will function according to the principle of collective consultation and collaboration with labour (*umfassende Mitwirkung der Werktätigen*), all in the spirit, of course, of 'democratic centralism'.[5] This is to be done with the objective of securing the creative initiative of combine workers in planning and management.

The current Soviet insistence on the financial independence and responsibility of production associations and enterprises, or 'self-financing' (*samofinansirovanie*), was also a high priority of GDR combine legislation. The latter decreed that in their self-financing (*Selbstfinanzierung*) practices, East German combines and enterprises must use credits received from banks with the greatest possible effectiveness.[6] The same holds, of course, for the funds generated internally, which are to be used for state levies, investments, and bonuses.[7]

As is true of *perestroika* for Soviet enterprises and associations, GDR plan perfecting foresaw greater pricing prerogatives for their industrial producers, the combines. This was to proceed, of course, under centrally determined guidelines and regulations, and was less bold than current Soviet pricing conceptions; but the combines nevertheless received the directive that they were to prepare and *implement* industrial pricing changes.[8] A final similarity worthy of mention was the expectation of GDR regulations that the

---

[4] *Gesetzblatt der Deutschen Demokratischen Republik*, 'Verordnung über die volkseigenen Kombinate, Kombinatsbetriebe und volkseigenen Betriebe', Teil 1 Nr. 38 (13 November 1979) p. 356.

[5] This socialist term is a euphemism pertaining to decision processes in socialism, under which the workers or citizens have every right to have their input, which then may be heeded or ignored when the decision is made at the centre.

[6] Ibid., p. 360.

[7] Ibid., p. 364.

[8] Ibid., p. 368.

combines would contribute in a major way to the health care and the cultural/social well being of the workers. Through contractual commitment of resources, combines and enterprises were to assist the local governments in developing and improving life in cities and towns, especially through the promotion of cultural, sport, social, and medical facilities.[9]

The dramatic difference between *perestroika* and GDR plan perfecting was the Soviet intention to effect a serious decentralization which would grant individual enterprises (not merely combines or production associations) much greater powers of decision. This would have been difficult for the East Germans to undertake back in 1979 and 1980, given their own inclinations and Soviet-imposed political constraints before Gorbachev.

The GDR seemed content to function well within those constraints, but did intend to relieve the over-burdened centre through a partial devolution of decision authority. They attempted this by granting expanded powers to the intermediate level of the planning hierarchy. The Directors General of the combines were permitted to share the responsibility for generating some planning balances and being involved in perspective planning tasks, which were to be performed on the basis of state planning coefficients and guidelines. The DGs were to disaggregate centrally developed branch plans for individual enterprises.[10]

Likewise, on the basis of legislation and central guidelines, Directors General were to determine what combine earnings levels would be achieved, to what level funds for the combine's economic and social purposes would be accumulated, and what share of member enterprise earnings would be transferred to the combine. They and the enterprise managers were to achieve effective utilization of productive resources and a systematic reduction of materials and energy in production.[11]

While finding the characteristics of a partial devolution of authority very satisfying, the East Germans failed to see (or

---

9 Ibid., p. 360.
10 Ibid., p. 357.
11 Ibid., p. 359.

didn't want to see) the shortcomings of this organization at the level of the enterprises within the *Kombinate*. The motivation of enterprise managers was very limited, since they were not permitted to take part in decision processes. They were without franchise when the combine's parent firm (also under the personal direction of the DG) co-opted effective operations, leaving inefficient ones under the jurisdiction of other enterprises. They were without voice as the assortment of consumer goods diminished, as the size of production units continued to grow, and as enterprise decision prerogatives were reduced.[12]

In concept, GDR plan-improving provisions of 1980 now seem less promising than the later, more comprehensive ones upon which reforms in the Soviet Union were to be based. But it is true of both the GDR and Soviet cases that the implementation of national economic policy is less progressive than one would expect from a reading of the enabling industrial regulations.

For the economists of Honecker's East Germany, who were intimately familiar with both the design and actual implementation of perestroika, it was difficult to see that Soviet devolution was substantively more progressive than their own measures, either in design or implementation. Gorbachev's 'Law on the State Enterprise' and the 'Law on Cooperatives' addressed Soviet problems in an important way, but during the Honecker era much still remained to be done to achieve a real restructuring of the entire system of economic management. For the economic mechanism to function properly, a comprehensive price reform, a well-functioning financial and banking system, an incentive-compatible set of indirect steering instruments, market-like economic behavior on the part of enterprise managers (*khozraschet*), a restructuring of the relations between central organs and enterprises (with the property rights of the latter clearly defined and unequivocally assured), and a functioning system of wholesale trade for the means of production, were all

---

[12] See Manfred Melzer, 'Die Rolle der Kombinate und Betriebe im Wirtschaftssystem der DDR', in Hans-Erich Grammatzki and Hans G. Nutzinger (eds), *Betrieb und Partizipation in Osteuropa* (Frankfurt/Main: Campus Verlag, 1986), pp. 445ff. See especially pp. 455–63.

unrealized necessary (but not necessarily sufficient) conditions for perestroika's success. An attempt to achieve some of these objectives was underway in the 1980s, and numerous changes had been scheduled for implementation over a several year period. The new ship of state had been launched, but it was not clear whether it had a steering mechanism.

There were two important differences in the actual functioning of the Soviet and East German economies. The first was the greater severity of Gorbachev's 'human factor' problem. In the GDR before the cataclysm, labour motivation was less of a problem than in the Soviet Union, even though their labour productivity lagged dramatically behind that of the Western countries. Moreover, the East German political system had remained quite stable over the past three-and-a-half decades. General Secretary Honecker claimed on several occasions that the GDR was a well-functioning socialist planning system that had proven itself to be 'productive, dynamic, and flexible'.[13]

The second fundamental difference was in the effectiveness of the economic planning organization in the two countries. Honecker's leadership claimed that the stable planning system of the GDR, founded on extremely large industrial organizations or conglomerates known as 'combines' (*Kombinate*),[14] was both effective and capable of realizing the possibilities of the

---

[13] See, for example, Erich Honecker, 'Die Aufgaben der Parteiorganisationen bei der weiteren Verwirklichung der Beschluesse des XI. Parteitages der SED', *Neues Deutschland*, 18 February 1987, p. 5.

[14] Combines are a form of both vertical (incorporating important resource-providing enterprises into the industry) and horizontal (uniting all final producers in the industry) integration. The authors have written extensively on the advantages and disadvantages of this organizational form, and some of these works will be cited later. For a most recent and brief treatment, see Bryson's, 'East German Traditional Centralism: An Alternative Route to Economic Reconstruction', *The Annals of the American Academy of Political and Social Science*, vol. 507 (January 1990), pp. 133–41. This work, also committed to final form just before the demise of the Honecker regime, also stands as a testament of the inability of social scientists to see into the future.

scientific-technical revolution.[15] As a result, the SED continually stressed its unwillingness to discuss fundamental changes in the system: the economic plan retained its effectiveness and, therefore, its dominance.[16]

THE HONECKER REGIME AND THE GORBACHEV REFORMS

The incompleteness and the uncertainties of the soviet reform drama explain at least in part why Honecker management was unwilling to launch its own versions of glasnost and perestroika. Its caution reflected the grave risks such dramatic change could represent for East Germany. How stable would the economic and social systems prove to be under fundamental change? Might thorough-going reform processes get out of control as the expectations and then the docility of the citizenry began to change? There was certainly no inclination to introduce market instruments into the system.

In a commentary on the 19th Party Conference of the CPSU, the GDR expressed great interest in and sympathy for the process of restructuring in the Soviet Union.[17] But it was also pointed out that every socialist party 'has to find solutions which take account of particular national conditions and requirements in the best possible way'.[18] In a visit to Moscow in September 1988, Honecker was told by Gorbachev that the recent strengthening of the Soviet leader's position in the Politburo had removed hindrances to reform, and the

---

[15] Gerd Friedrich, 'Kombinate:Rückgrat Sozialistischer Planwirtschaft', *Neues Deutschland*, 18 June 1987.

[16] Helmut Koziolek observed that 'the tasks fixed in the plan are law, they are obligatory for all sectors of responsibility down to the Kombinat and its enterprises'. See his article, 'Die Steigerung der Arbeitsproduktivität ist das Entscheidende für den Sieg der neuen Gesellschaft', *Wirtschaftswissenschaft*, Nr. 11 (1987) p. 1615.

[17] Die XIX Parteikonferenz der KPdSU und unser gemeinsamer Kampf für Frieden und Sozialismus', *Neues Deutschland*, 8 July 1988, p. 2.

[18] Ibid.

speed and extent of perestroika would be significant. In his response, Honecker expressed full sympathy and support, but emphasized that the GDR would be carrying on its own strategy of 'the unity of social and economic policy', pursuing the reforms mandated by that policy.[19]

Having examined the initial philosophy and organization of combine formation in the GDR and perestroika in the USSR, we wish to review briefly the SED position on these two fundamentally different approaches to reform. The perestroika approach assumes that the necessary industrial structure can be achieved when one changes the management system, extends market relations, builds up competition, and adjusts other such elements of the economic plan. The GDR believed that the industrial structure must be determined in advance; it placed high value on what it believed would be the 'key technologies' over the next decade, and had worked out a strategy for their development to the year 2000. This became the starting point from which step by step changes of the economic mechanism were to be made. This strategy, which the GDR considered superior, was the basis for the refusal to adopt perestroika.

This was not, of course, the only reason for the GDR's reluctance to embrace Soviet-style reform. Others included the desire to wait and see how things continued to develop in the Soviet Union. Waiting permitted learning: what wrong steps might one be able to avoid, and what sequencing changes might make the individual reform initiatives more effective should a more dramatic reform concept have to be developed later? What this posture missed was simply that the GDR's actual economic situation urgently required new reform initiatives.

When the Hungarians refused to cooperate in keeping East Germans captive within their own country (mid-1989), and once the Soviets made it clear that they would no longer help block the flight of the disenchanted, there was little room left for ameliorative action on the part of the party. With the increasing stream of refugees, the economic future of the country turned from uncertain to serious.

---

[19] *Neues Deutschland*, 29 September 1988, p. 2.

Honecker lacked the capacity to respond and the party was unable to conceive of any effective adjustments to the crisis.

TIES BETWEEN SOVIET AND EAST GERMAN PLANNING

The GDR's 'streamlined administrative structure built around *Kombinate*' and the readily observable 'continual push for additional mergers and superministerial-type organs' have not escaped the attention of experts on the Soviet economy.[20] But there is more to notice. Organizational developments in East German industry going into the 1980s were the result of the GDR's complete willingness, prior to the Gorbachev era, to accept and adopt the planning measures and strategies of the Soviet Union; the combine movement itself began on initiatives and concepts originating in the Soviet Union.[21]

Through the history of GDR-Soviet relations, the East Germans were expected to remain conversant with the party line from Moscow and to follow it with alacrity. Accordingly, all through the Brezhnev era the Honecker regime 'loyally' followed even the implicit suggestions of the Soviet partner. In the case of combine organization, it simply implemented the party line from Moscow with an effectiveness which the Soviets could not duplicate.

Unavoidable ties to the Soviet Union were in part responsible for the development of East Germany's rather highly centralized economic planning system. When those institutions succeeded, however, in taking on a quasi-viable form in the GDR, it became difficult for the East Germans to change course and discard the old ways.

Frequent and detailed communications have long been extant in various forms between the Soviet and East German economics

---

[20] See, for example, Hewett, E. A., (1988), *Reforming the Soviet Economy: Equality versus Efficiency* (Washington, D. C.: The Brookings Institution) pp. 300, 301.

[21] See G. Schneider and M. Troeder, *Zur Genesis der Kombinate der zentralgeleiteten Industrie in der Deutschen DR.* Berichte des Osteuropa-Instituts an der Freien Universitaet Berlin, Reihe Wirtschaft und Recht, No. 137 (1985) Berlin [West].

intelligentsia. These contacts were regularized in 1974 with the formation of an important facilitative institution, the Joint Commission of Economists of the USSR and GDR, which met regularly for extensive discussion of basic planning problems and economic developments. Graupner *et al.*[22] speak of the achievement of a qualitatively new stage in GDR history with the establishment of the Joint Commission.

Over the history of this institution, associated Soviet and East German economists have been jointly concerned with problems such as the following:

- intensification of socialist expanded reproduction and increasing its efficiency,
- the economic and social ramifications of technical progress,
- the improvement of management and planning systems,
- the promotion of more effective socialist economic integration,
- the 'socialist world system in revolutionary world processes',
- combining science and production in Soviet and GDR industry,
- the agro-industrial complexes and intensifying their production, and
- the effective utilization of social labour.

According to published reports, discussions of the commission were in unanimous agreement that science and technology are key factors in the pursuit of intensification. Hastening technical progress has decisive significance in achieving the economic objectives of the party, especially in assuring the development of the socialist personality and society. Ideas about how to achieve shared goals are investigated at the Commission's meetings in detail.

But the formal interaction of Soviet and East German economists is not limited to the Commission. Other important avenues include,

---

22 See K.-H. Graupner, E. Schmidt, and G. Vogel, '15 Jahre Wissenschaftlicher Rat Für die wirtschaftswissenschaftliche Forschung bei der Akademie der Wissenschaften der DDR', *Wirtschaftswissenschaft*, 35, No. 10 (1987) pp. 1441–5.

for example, continuous GDR exposure to Soviet publications in the original and through translations, professional interaction through university research, CMEA joint planning activities, and so on. GDR economists were always very familiar with the current thinking of their Soviet colleagues.

A fascinating example of the common origins of Soviet/East German economic thought is worthy of mention. The economics establishments of both countries shared the conviction that in the reform process one of the fundamental errors of the 1960s reforms must be avoided. Gorbachev is on record to the effect that the fundamental error of the economic reform of the sixties was that organizational change proceeded from the top down. According to him:

. . . perhaps the chief shortcoming was that we began from the top. One might think that this is logical for a planned economy. But this time we have decided to begin everything with the main unit, because as soon as we undertook to examine questions of planning and management at the level of the central agencies, there was nothing left for the enterprise. The upper levels took everything for themselves. No cardinal measures were forthcoming. The new provisions and recommendations reached enterprises in a halfhearted, curtailed form, and we were never able to really get this process under way and bring it home to people's minds, to bring it to a logical conclusion. Therefore, in the 1960s and 1970s the reform and our efforts to improve economic management did not produce a full effect.[23]

A full year earlier, on 16 May, the Director of the Central Institute of Economics of the Academy of Sciences of the GDR, Wolfgang Heinrichs, had already made the following very interesting statement at a workshop on the GDR Economy in Washington DC:

---

23 See M. Gorbachev, 'Party Meeting Previews Economic Reform', *The Current Digest of the Soviet Press*, 39, No. 24 (15 July 1987) pp. 1–4. A talk reported in Pravda, 10 June 1987, p. 1.

In the 1960s the socialist government of the GDR wanted to reform economic management. (I worked for the government at that time.) We began reform at the top level. We started by listing the different tasks for the Council of Ministers, the Central Planning commission and the Regional Bodies. Then we realized that most tasks had already been assigned, and that few were left over for the enterprises. As you know, this reform was not successful, and it was abandoned for other reasons. From this we learned that we must start at the bottom, not the top. This is a fundamentally different solution for a centrally planned economy – to assign tasks from the bottom up.[24]

In spite of the rhetoric, however, starting from the bottom up was the last thing the GDR really wished to do. Granting the individual enterprises substantially increased rights might have encouraged them to begin a dialogue focussing on the inefficiency of the past economic decisions of the centre. Next, this potential use of economic power for political purposes might be employed to cast doubts on some of the centre's political decisions. Fearing, therefore, that tension and discontent might grow through decentralization and that they might not have the means of containing it, they simply opted not to decentralize.

GDR LOYALTY TO THE OLD WAY

One striking example of East German responsiveness to Soviet direction was related in an interview[25] with a resentful GDR economist. In about 1970, as a part of an earlier East German reform program, the 'New Economic System of Planning and Economic Management', experience with half-nationalized, half-private GDR

---

[24] See W. Heinrichs, 'Comments' ('Symposium on the German Democratic Republic), *Comparative Economic Studies*, 29, No. 2 (Summer, 1987) pp. 54–61.

[25] The interview with W. Heinrichs was conducted by Bryson as a part of a research exchange stay in Berlin (East) in June 1989.

enterprises had seemed very promising. The Soviets considered this ownership arrangement, however, as a violation of the principles of socialist property relations. They simply ordered the East Germans to reorganize (nationalize) their half-private enterprises at once.

Nearly two decades later, the Soviet reform attempt began to address the economic disaster that their traditional property and ownership ideology had helped to create. They attempted to overcome the problem by legalizing and proclaiming the glories of private cooperatives. Now Soviet pressure on the GDR was reversed; Berlin was expected to get started at once on this new method of privatization.

There is no question that the Honecker administration was anything but comfortable with the increasing pressures perestroika brought to bear. Gorbachev clearly had the conviction that glasnost is a matter not only for the Soviets, but for socialists in general, although he was not given to expressing his viewpoint in the form of a policy prescription for the brother countries. He neither pressured hard-line East European socialists to reform, nor did he oppose their dismissal after they had continually refused to follow his lead.

There is, however, a certain irony in the pressure that ultimately brought about the Honecker demise. For a period of 15 years after the termination of the reforms of the sixties, while progressive forces in Hungary and Poland were clearly anxious to achieve the greatest possible liberalization, the East Germans stood loyally by Brezhnev's Soviets, faithfully implementing and, in their own view, even achieving a basic mastery of the methodology of central planning. Suddenly there was pressure to conform to a development path which, for Honecker's tastes, was a revisionistic one. He abhorred that path to the end.

THE GDR'S STRATEGY FOR AVOIDING PERESTROIKA

Other things being equal, one would have expected pressures from Moscow to succeed in 'inspiring' a fundamental alteration of the economic mechanism. Yet one would also expect GDR socialism to attempt to retain its own credibility and viability (including that of its general secretary) from any perceived threat, domestic or international. As long as Honecker kept surviving, people considered him a 'survivor'; he was able to do so for a time because he endeavored to perform his foot-dragging in a creative way. Since perestroika was an unacceptable strategy for Honecker and his lieutenants, they tried to avoid it without offending the Soviets or inciting unrest among their own people. Avoiding perestroika became the strategy of the SED.

In the last of the Honecker years, the SED was loathe to criticize Soviet-style reform. To find fault with socialism's foremost power had always been dangerous. Honecker ascended to SED leadership when the abrasiveness of his predecessor, Walter Ulbricht, proved excessive for Soviet tastes. Honecker did not forget that lesson, but was ultimately no more successful than Ulbricht in trying to stay abreast of a changing Soviet-bloc world.

The intelligentsia of the Honecker regime could see no point in embracing Soviet-style reform prematurely. That too could be risky. Should perestroika fail in the Soviet Union, an investment by the GDR in similar reforms (in terms both of costly organizational and policy changes) might largely be wasted. More importantly, any changes inspired by perestroika could represent a political liability after the fact.

It was not necessary, of course, for perestroika irrevocably to succeed before adoption would be safe. Many observers are convinced that some form of reform package, whether or not under the perestroika label, would persist in the Soviet Union even if Gorbachev were to disappear from the scene.[26] If that expectation held in Honecker's East Germany, the SED would have been prudent to publicize (as a PR gesture addressed at the Soviets) the adoption of any policies with the remotest flavour of openness or economic

---

[26] The reorganization of the politburo in October 1988, which conferred the presidency formerly held by the retired Gromyko on Gorbachev, and which transferred Ligachev from ideology to agriculture, made it appear that the General Secretary was still managing opposition to his reforms. Later reorganizations likewise indicated that despite Western pessimism, he was keeping power well managed.

reconstruction. That would have given the appearance of compliance without incurring its costs.

Naturally, the East Germans had considerable motivation to continue to pursue improvements in their planning system independent of Soviet reform pressures. Of necessity attention continued to be given to improving the economic mechanism. But to delay the really radical and costly kinds of change, and to implement them only gradually, might minimize problems arising from the sequencing of reforms. The timing of major and complex facets of systemic change can be very difficult. Consider, for example, the hazards of granting greater responsibility to production units for cost accounting and self-financing *before* introducing needed price reform. How can one know, without scarcity prices (those reflecting actual supplies and demands), whether a production unit's performance deserves praise or censure? Without adequate prices, 'profitability' may accompany poor performance and 'losses' may accompany what would otherwise be commendable achievement. Likewise, resorting to *khozraschet* and self-financing would logically precede appropriate changes in the system of centrally directed supply. Waiting would permit a 'second-wave' reform movement to profit from the experience of more progressive pioneers. The observation of reform problems and solutions elsewhere would be of assistance in the implementation and sequencing of GDR reforms.

Regardless of its motives in the Gorbachev era, the GDR cannot fairly be accused of consistent opposition to reform in general. Both during and after the reform of the sixties, the East Germans had consistently maintained that adjusting the economic mechanism must be an ongoing, open-ended process. Reform was seen as a continual, creative search for effective solutions to new tasks and challenges.[27] The advantages of socialism should be exploited and publicized with their country-specific, concrete characteristics. Plan perfecting and 'in some countries even reconstruction or reform'[28]

---

[27] H.-G. Haupt, and K. Hövelmans, 'Zu ausgewählten Entwicklungsproblemen des sozialistischen Weltsystems', *Wirtschaftswissenschaft*, 36, No. 7 (1988) pp. 961–77.
[28] Ibid., pp. 969–70.

of the economic mechanism was an important component of this process.

Clearly, the creative search for optimal solutions undertaken by different Marxist-Leninist parties results in vastly diverse methodologies for similar problems. Every country penetrates new frontiers and there are no general panaceas. According to Honecker, the SED moved forward and adopted new methods as necessary. It separated itself from those things which did not prove successful, and retained those which did. 'For we are communists,' he proclaimed, 'and, as Lenin expressed it, the party of innovators.'[29]

The GDR's ideological hard sell of *Planvervollkommnung* (both to the East German people and the Soviets) included an implicit rejection of the Hungarian way.[30] Nor were the Chinese reforms (before retrenchment) deemed worthy of emulation; the Chinese had borrowed heavily from the Hungarians. And it goes without saying that for Honecker's tastes perestroika (which in some respects draws more than just inspiration from the Hungarian model) also bore the weakness of too little central direction.

Heinrichs, a leading East German economist, has suggested that casual western observation failed to perceive the substantive changes that had occurred in the East German economy. Western economists believed Hungarian change to be more dramatic, which in his view was simply erroneous. He says:

> We often hear the opinion that the Hungarian experiment was effective because of its market orientation. Our Western colleagues compare the GDR to the Hungarian standard. The Hungarian experiment has several interesting aspects in the opinion of many GDR economists. What we evaluate positively is how

---

29 See E. Honecker, *Mit dem Volk und für das Volk realisieren wir die Generallinie unserer Partei zum Wohle der Menschen. Aus dem Referat des Generalsekretärs des Zentralkommitees der SED und Vorsitzenden des Staatsrates der DDR auf der Beratung des Zentralkomitees mit den 1. Sekretären der Kreisleitungen am 12. Februar 1988* (Berlin [East]: Dietz Verlag, 1988) p. 17.
30 Kornai, J., 'The Hungarian Reform Process', *Journal of Economic Literature*, 24, No. 4 (December 1986) pp. 1687–737.

they use price and market mechanisms, especially for consumer goods. On the other hand, we do not overlook the increasing social differentiation triggered by this mechanism. I only use this example to say we should prepare ourselves for long-term learning and draw upon all the experience accumulated by other socialist nations. This should lead to a further re-evaluation of what we have done. Among the socialist nations there are no longer teachers and pupils, masters and apprentices as it once was. We are learning together. It is important for our Western colleagues to recognize this.[31]

It is true that journalists in that period tended largely to glamorize the Hungarian case and ignore the progress of the GDR.

Gorbachev himself applied little direct pressure on Honecker's Socialist Unity Party (SED) to adopt perestroika, and the East Germans were confident enough to develop a plausible rationale for avoiding the speed and extensiveness of the reform movements of the Soviets, Hungarians, and Poles. In interviews,[32] this rationalization was articulated effectively by GDR economists roughly as follows:

It is true that Perestroika *must* succeed if socialism is to survive, but the USSR is now an equal partner, and the GDR is confident that it is completely free to choose its own way. The old thesis of the unification (convergence) of socialist systems was false; national differences do *not* become less significant over time. The USSR was once the economic development model for the other socialist countries, but at the same time, there was also a German path to socialism. It involved, for example, private land and private handicrafts. The GDR industrial enterprise was always a legal entity functioning according to the principles of

---

[31] See Heinrichs, 'Comments', *op. cit.*, pp. 55, 56.
[32] These were conducted in the spring of 1989, thanks to a grant from the International Research and Exchanges Board and the Ministry for Higher Education of the GDR.

economic accounting. A new thesis has now been proposed: socialist development leads to more divergent forms.

But while this rationale was being developed by the intelligentsia and the party, the message of Gorbachev on reform effectively transmitted rising expectations to East German citizens. They had for too long been exposed to the slogan that became anathema to Honecker in his last years: 'To learn from the Soviet Union is to learn victory'.

There was still some uncertainty about launching reforms of Gorbachev's type, given the fact that the East Germans kept receiving the implicit message that their system was performing substantially better than that of the Soviets. The Honecker leadership had learned from the New Economic System of the 1960s that the reform route was extremely arduous and fraught with uncertain outcomes. It would require extensive price revisions and a demanding price reform, embracing the very nature of price formation. It would require overcoming the problems in neglected sectors after excessive attention had been lavished upon the structure-determining (later 'key technology') industries. The basic problems could be addressed much more easily through combines than through a system decentralizing authority to innumerable, smaller firms. Indeed, the response to perestroika had been made in the GDR before that concept evolved in the Soviet Union; it was combine formation and the whole complex of plan-perfecting measures of the early 1980s. East Germany had made the proper inferences from their own *New Economic System* of the 1960s. Why couldn't the Soviets do so?

The rationale might have seemed convincing to the party, but it was an empty political debate to the East German people. While the party lauded its own record, the people waited in sullen dissatisfaction. The opening of the GDR's borders revealed clearly for the first time the serious errors that ultimately led to the collapse of the Honecker regime:

1. Neither the General Secretary nor his close associates recognized that glasnost in the USSR would have a dramatic, far-reaching impact on other East European regimes. The interdiction even on

the discussion of existing problems or of potential solutions and the impossibility of political activity beyond the very restrictive party line imposed from above, led to considerable and growing dissatisfaction and hostility in the GDR citizenry.

2. The GDR leadership failed to give sufficient consideration to the fact that the denial of exit visas permitting emigration had caused tension and pressure that were becoming explosive. In a moment of confidence about the achievements of socialism, the government announced in 1984 that any citizens who wanted to cope with the possibilities of joblessness, inflation, homelessness, etc. in West Germany could just go ahead and apply for exit visas. The applications were surprisingly numerous until, after only a few months, the government changed the policy. Once again, getting out of the GDR became as hard as ever – until the sudden collapse at the end of 1989.

The behaviour of the East Germans from the autumn of 1989 on demonstrated that the citizenry basically considered itself imprisoned behind the wall. That was not the image the GDR had presented of itself before that time, nor was that image clearly perceived by scholars or journalists, who in turn painted the West's intellectual image of East Germany.

3. The favourable economic developments of the first half of the 1980s had made the GDR leadership too self-confident by the second half of the decade. They became convinced that they had mastered the basic techniques of economic planning and could indefinitely achieve steady growth and technical progress. But was the assertion of economic progress in East Germany a credible one? By the late 1980s it was becoming evident that economic development was not progressing as had been anticipated. While some East European countries attempted to implement economic reforms, the East Germans continued to try various 'refinements'. They did so until the optimism and confidence of the early 1980s dissipated in the storms of social upheaval.

2 GDR Economic Performance in the Final Honecker Years

GDR PLANNING REPUTATION AND PERFORMANCE

By the mid-1980s the GDR was confident that it had developed solutions to most of the basic problems of central planning. As almost all of the socialist bloc countries struggled with economic stagnation, the East Germans continued to maintain respectable growth rates. With the exception of the GDR, there appeared in the mid-eighties to be no East European socialist country capable of the peremptory solution of any significant economic problem. Difficulties that demanded adaptation ranging from 'radical reform' to minor and spontaneous policy change reappeared again and again on planning agendas. Proposed solutions often seemed familiar – primarily because they, too, cycled and recycled through public discussion, specialized literatures, and legislation. Only the GDR seemed capable of refining the planning mechanism; it was regarded as the most effectively functioning of the socialist planned economies.

Toward the conclusion of the Honecker era, however, East German optimism about the future of the planning system had become far less robust. The reappearance around 1987 of seemingly insoluble problems cast doubts on the durability of the 'plan-perfecting' exercise of the 1980s and it was no longer possible to assume that the surprisingly strong East German economic performance would continue.[1]

---

[1] See Doris Cornelsen, 'Die Lage der DDR-Wirtschaft zur Jahreswende 1987–88', *Wochenbericht*, Deutsches Institut Für Wirtschaftsforschung, no. 5 (1988).

In this chapter we wish to investigate the East German claims of planning success; we will find instances of solid achievement, of course, but will also find significant areas of inadequacy and a growing need for reform. We will consider first the economic performance of the last three years of the Honecker era, then discuss the planning strategy and organization underlying that performance.

ECONOMIC DEVELOPMENTS OF 1987

Significant difficulties began with the effects of a severe winter in the first quarter of 1987; it strained energy supplies and caused problems in the transport sector. Shortages spread through the entire economy, and the resultant effects were worse than could be inferred from the reported national income growth of 3.6 per cent for the year (plan target, 4.5 per cent). Manufacturing, especially in the chemical industry, lagged far behind plan targets. Consumer goods supplies did not remain unaffected, and frequent complaints were heard about tardy supply deliveries and the product mix.[2] Nor could the level of foreign trade achieved in the early 1980s be maintained. Net private money incomes of the population increased more than did supplies of consumer goods. These worrisome developments could certainly not be blamed on weather problems alone. Increasing miseries were also related, firstly, to the investment sector, which was sharply criticized by East German specialists, and, secondly, to the insufficient upgrading – both qualitative and technological – of manufactured products.

The investment plan for 1987 called for a small reduction in capital investments, but in fact investment expenditures grew by six percent. This specious improvement was actually a negative development, since the expansion of capital did not increase productive capacity at all.

---

[2] See, for example, *Ostsee-Zeitung*, 16 September 1987; *Lausitzer Rundschau*, 17 September 1987; *Schweriner Volkszeitung*, 17 September 1987.

According to the plan, three quarters of the planned increase in output was to be achieved through new investment. Politburo member Felfe admitted[3] that 751 investment projects were not completed on schedule, which caused serious bottlenecks in important sectors. The delays were blamed on insufficient preparation and project development, which were a result of difficulties in the construction industry. Building capacities were spread over too many projects, equipment was generally dilapidated and obsolete, and building materials (too often exported in response to international debt and trade balance problems) were in short supply. Honecker criticized the minister of the construction sector for merely 'getting used to delays' in project completion;[4] he mentioned regions where construction achievements were less than 80 per cent of the plan (Berlin, Rostock), or only between 80 and 90 per cent (Suhl and Karl-Marx-Stadt). Unfortunately, other deficiencies remained as well. Because the failure of a single component could bring robots and other automated equipment to a standstill, it was emphasized continually that the introduction of key technologies must be quicker and the standards of performance higher.[5] In addition to the internal production problems, there were also shortfalls in the deliveries of essential inputs from CMEA partners.

With regard to product upgrading, Honecker commented in review of the 1987 plan year that 32 per cent of manufacturing's net profit (12.5 billion Marks; hereafter, for notational convenience, M12.5 billion) had been generated by new products. The share of new products in exports to the West increased in 1987 from 36 to 42 per cent. But he warned that these statistics should not deceive anybody; the important breakthrough in quality had not yet been achieved.[6]

An important target of Party Congress XI was that 60 per cent

---

3 Werner Felfe, 'Aus dem Bericht des Politbüros an die 5. Tagung des ZK der SED', *Neues Deutschland*, 17 December 1987, p. 6.

4 Erich Honecker, 'Mit dem Volk' *op. cit*, pp. 29–30.

5 See Guenter Mittag, *Mit der Kraft der Kombinate weiter voran auf dem Weg des XI Parteitags. Seminar des ZK der SED mit den Generaldirektoren der Kombinate und den Parteiorganisationen des ZK am 10. und 11. März, 1988 in Leipzig* (Berlin [East], 1988) pp. 65, 66.

6 Erich Honecker, 'Mit dem Volk' *op. cit*, pp. 27, 28.

of the GDR's final consumer goods would have achieved top international quality levels by 1990. But that level was far too optimistic, since enterprises were still insufficiently motivated to implement innovations and produce quality products. For the first two years after the introduction of new or acceptably improved products, the *Kombinate* and enterprises were to be granted much higher profit earnings; thereafter the price was to be systematically reduced. A product was considered 'new', however, even if only a quarter of its 'use-value' was substantially upgraded. Hence, slight changes in colour, equipment, or other characteristics qualified the producer for the higher returns. With these standards, it was no wonder planners were determined that the production of commodities with 'quality' labels should increase more rapidly than total product.

But things were not all black for consumers in 1987. An increase in family subsidies after May 1 applied for the whole year. There were also wage increases and performance-related bonuses in health and social services, for teachers and educators, police and other security forces.

ECONOMIC DEVELOPMENTS OF 1988

Performance in the first half of 1988 was not better than it had been in 1987.[7] It is true that a growth of national income of 4.1 per cent, corresponding to plan targets, was reported. That, however, merely veiled real developments. Although the winter ushering in 1988 was mild in comparison to that of the previous year, the first quarter's growth should have been higher. With two more working days in the first half of 1988, the adjusted growth rate from 1987 was only 2.5 per cent .

The year's overall results were disappointing, because it had been billed quite correctly as a decisive year for the fulfilment of the five-year plan 1986–90. This is apparent from the data

[7] See Doris Cornelsen, 'DDR-Wirtschaft im ersten Halbjahr 1988', *DIW Wochenbericht*, no. 30, 1988.

TABLE 2.1 *GDR Economic Indicators*
(Percentage Growth Rates)

	1986	1987	1988
Produced National Income	4.3	3.6	2.7
Industrial Goods	4.3	3.7	3.7
Agriculture			
Plant Production	–3.0	3.2	–11.0
Meat Production	3.0	0.6	0.1
Retail Sales	4.1	3.6	3.9
Foodstuffs	2.8	3.1	2.1
Industrial Goods	5.4	4.2	5.7
Foreign Trade Turnover	1.0	–3.0	0.3
Imports	4.3	–4.2	0.4
Exports	–2.1	–1.7	0.1
Net Cash Receipts of Populace	4.5	4.7	3.9
Investments	5.3	8.0	5.0

SOURCE: *Data here are taken from a more complete set provided by Cornelsen, 'Lage zur Jahreswende 1988/89', op. cit., p. 54.*

in Table 2.1. Production was falling further and further behind and the economy began to function under more difficult conditions: labour, energy and materials had become more scarce, production facilities were frequently obsolescent, and the anticipated effects from improvements in science and technology were not experienced.[8]

A number of the continuing problems were a consequence of the capital goods deficit that developed in the period of the credit crisis and continued thereafter. In order to sustain the export drive of that period, without having to cut too deeply into consumer goods supplies, investments were scaled back sharply. As a result, many parts of the capital stock were in severe need of replacement and modernization, and continuous repairs became very costly.

Securing more abundant volumes of the labour, energy, and raw materials in short supply would have required substantial investments. In statistics on national income use the share of

---

[8] Doris Cornelsen, *op cit*, 1989, p. 53.

investments sank from a high of 24 per cent in 1978 to less than 18 per cent in 1985, but began to rise again thereafter. In 1987 it was barely 19 per cent, although it grew in real terms by 5 per cent in 1988.[9] By that time the need to invest could no longer be ignored.

The problems of inadequate preparation for the tardy completion of investment projects continued to plague overall economic performance. When planned new capacities were not forthcoming, enterprises whose input plans were based on growth expectations failed to reach their targets. Their shortfalls then proceeded to spread through other interdependent sectors of the economy.[10]

The same problem applied, of course, to the production of consumer goods. Some branches suffered from long delays and severe shortages in numerous of the commodities and services provided by the regionally directed combines, which typically stock grocery stores.[11] Some shortages in department stores were also attributable to the export drive, and these difficulties were exacerbated by inept and slow decision processes on the part of ministries and enterprise directors.[12]

Overall performance in consumer goods provision was rather mixed. In 1988 housing targets were, as often before, 'overfulfilled', as the GDR moved to the end of a long campaign to provide adequate housing for all citizens. Although the GDR was fully prepared to claim its targets reached and the housing programme a success, housing clearly remained a problem for diappointingly long lists of frustrated applicants. There were still serious problems

---

[9] See ibid, p. 55.
[10] Politburo member Kurt Hager complained in June 1988 that the construction and assembling combines of Magdeburg, Erfurt and Frankfurt, the metalworks combine of Leipzig, and the special construction combine for water supply in Weimar must all find measures to increase output and to complete all planned projects with good quality by the arranged completion date. See *Aus dem Bericht des Politbüros an das ZK der SED* (Berlin [East], 1988) p. 34.
[11] See Günter Schabowski, 'Verantwortungsbewußtes Handeln auf dem Weg des XI. Parteitages', *Neues Deutschland*, 17 September 1988, p. 3.
[12] See Dieter Resch, 'Besseres Angebot verlangt Einsatz aller Betriebe', *Berliner Zeitung*, 24 October 1988, p. 3.

concerning the modernization of the older portions of the housing stock; vast repairs were – and are – still required and the inner cities remained in need of extensive remodelling. Some housing shortfalls can be explained, of course, by an upward trend in incomes and expectations and by increases in the number of small households, but a severe shortage of larger units with four or more rooms continued. These limitations will remain substantial for some time unless West German assistance is addressed to GDR housing.

The supply of textiles, home electronic goods, shoes, sport articles, furniture, and 'the thousand small items' required by households suffered some gaps right to the end of the Honecker era. Increasing incomes did permit 7 per cent sales increases in *Delikatläden* (speciality, higher quality clothing shops), partially compensating for shortfalls in normal consumer goods production.

ECONOMIC DEVELOPMENTS OF 1989

For the 1989 plan, serious problems were encountered in the preparation of the balance sheets. Planning participants were warned to take care that plan targets, balances for materials, and planned investment expenditures be in equilibrium.[13] For some sectors of the economy available inputs were of insufficient quantity and quality. The economic plan for the GDR's fortieth year of existence was thus endangered even before it appeared. The need for substantially improved economic performance cried out for new reform measures.

In the period directly preceding the cataclysm, the GDR's most significant endeavours to effect change related to investments. With a new law effected at the beginning of 1989, large projects became a part of a state plan for investments.[14] The plan included 300

---

[13] See Resch, ibid.
[14] See 'Verordnung über die Planung, Bildung, und Verwendung der Investionsfonds', *Gesetzblatt der DDR*, Teil I, 30. November 1988, pp. 279ff.

important projects of structural importance; in 1989 these represented about a fifth of total investments and nearly a third of industrial investments.[15] All combines and enterprises in industry and construction were to adopt the principle of self-responsibility for investment funds. The program began in sixteen experimental combines, which were to receive substantially increased decision prerogatives. At a later point we will return to these increased rights.

THE BASIS OF GDR PERFORMANCE: 'PLAN PERFECTING' IN THE EARLY 1980s

Having abandoned a reform attempt to return in 1970 to central planning and its attendant inflexibility, inefficiency, and low productivity,[16] and having experienced in the 1970s two energy crises and declining terms of trade on the international front,[17] the GDR faced the necessity of developing a new economic strategy for the 1980s.[18] Such a strategy would have to enhance labour-saving methods of production and increase savings of energy, materials, and capital. The strategy chosen was to be implemented through two important processes, a 'combine reform' and a series of legislative and

---

[15] See *Presse-Informationen*, 11 April 1989, p. 2.
[16] See Manfred Melzer, 'Probleme und voraussichtliche Entwicklung der Industrie in der DDR', *Vierteljahrshefte zur Wirtschaftsforschung des DIW*, no. 3/4 (1980) pp. 361ff.
[17] For more details see Doris Cornelsen, 'Hauptaufgabe Export – Die Direktive zum Fünfjahrplan für die Wirtschaft der DDR 1981 bis 1985', *Wochenbericht des DIW*, no. 31 (1981).
[18] For a more detailed treatment, see Phillip J. Bryson and Manfred Melzer, *Planning Refinements and Combine Formation in East German Economic 'Intensification'*, The Carl Beck Papers in Russian and East European Studies, University of Pittsburgh, 508: pp. 19–23 (1986). See also Manfred Melzer and Arthur A. Stahnke, 'The GDR Faces the Economic Dilemmas of the 1980s: Caught between the Need for New Methods and Restricted Options', *East European Economies: Slow Growth in the 1980s*, vol. 3 (Washington, D.C.: Joint Economic Committee of the Congress of the United States, 1986), pp. 131–68.

organizational changes designed to improve the planners' indirect and direct 'steering' of the economy.

The Kombinat Reform

From 1979 to 1982 the GDR reorganized its economy on the basis of industrial combines (*Kombinate*).[19] As the Honecker era came to an end, 126 centrally directed combines employed an average of 25,000 workers in some twenty to forty enterprises. There were, in addition, 95 regionally directed combines of smaller size, generally producing consumer goods. The GDR hoped these vertically and horizontally integrated groups of enterprises would bring several advantages, for example, an acceleration of scientific and technical progress, improved supply conditions, more efficient use of machinery, lower production costs, and improvement of product assortments and quality through appropriate innovation. It was intended that the combines would rationalize production, create larger production units with better internal organization, reduce interbranch and intersectoral coordination problems for the ministries, and initiate more flexible planning and more effective decision-making processes.

The enterprises retained their legal independence, although they became very dependent upon the Director General (DG) of the combine. The latter enjoyed significant prerogatives, including those of reassigning production capacities and leadership roles in all the combine's enterprises.[20] The DG not only directed the combine, but also became the manager of the 'parent enterprise' (*Stammbetrieb*) of that industrial branch; he became, therefore, both a ministerial agent and an entrepreneur, and was enjoined to introduce new

---

[19] See Manfred Melzer, Angela Scherzinger, and Cord Schwartau, 'Wird das Wirtschaftssystem der DDR durch vermehrte Kombinatsbildung effizienter', *Vierteljahrshefte zur Wirtschaftsforschung des DIW*, no. 4 (1979) pp. 365ff. See also Phillip J. Bryson and Manfred Melzer: 'The Kombinat in GDR Economic Orginization', in Ian Jeffries and Manfred Melzer (eds), *The East German Economy* (London: Croom Helm, 1987), pp. 51–68.
[20] Verordnung über die volkseigenen Kombinate, Kombinatsbetriebe und volkseigenen Betriebe', *Gesetzblatt der DDR*, Part I (1979) pp. 355ff.

technologies, to penetrate new markets, and to achieve 'intensification' (to increase production through improved technologies and increased labour productivity rather than through the utilization of more extensive volumes of labour and capital).

The 'Perfecting' of Direct and Indirect Steering

In 1982 and 1983 GDR economic leaders introduced a 'flood' of new planning directives, improved management techniques, and planning coefficients. These new 'steering mechanisms', together with combine formation, were designed to achieve intensification of production. It was hoped that greater precision in central planning and a strengthening of cost-benefit thinking on the part of managers would assure improved performance. Evaluating enterprises and combines on the basis of profitability was also intended to stimulate greater productivity and cost discipline.[21]

With regard to direct steering, about 90 planning indicators were adopted in 1984, but only four of them were regarded as really significant: net production, net profit, products and services for the population, and exports. These were to replace the long-criticized gross output measure, 'industrial commodity production', which would have continued to guarantee the waste of materials and the delivery of poor quality outputs.[22] In this period the balancing of raw materials and semi-finished products was further developed; the central planning organs generated 2,136 balances, determining

---

[21] See Manfred Melzer, 'The New Planning and Steering Mechanisms in the GDR: Between Pressure for Efficiency and Success in "Intensification" Policy', *Studies in Comparative Communism*, no. 1 (1987) pp. 9–25.

[22] It has proved impossible in central planning to set plan targets based on gross output which are significantly specific to elicit the proper production response. For example, when enterprises are rewarded for producing a volume of windows based on weight, produced glass becomes heavy and very thick. When planners attempt to correct this (setting as the target a total output measured in square metres), the glass produced then tends to be extensive in area, but so thin that it crumbles on the way to the production site. The problem is, of course, that the producer feels the desirable commodity characteristics are ignored when the ministry is only interested in the growth of physical production.

76 percent of industrial inputs; a further 2,400 balances were drawn up by the combines themselves.[23]

In the effort to achieve indirect steering, the role of net revenues was upgraded to become the criterion for rational resource utilization. Also, levies influencing net profit (e.g., the production fund levy, net profit deduction, and regulations for the formation and use of enterprise funds) were altered. The 'contribution for social funds' (*Beitrag für gesellschaftliche Fonds*) was an important innovation of this period; the imposition of a huge payroll tax – amounting to 70 per cent of the total wages fund – was intended to force enterprises to economize on (rather than hoard) labour.

A price markup was introduced for goods awarded the 'quality' label, and much higher profits were allowed for goods sold in the *Exquisit* and *Delikat* shops. For obsolete goods, price *reductions* were implemented. The prices of new products were thereafter determined on the basis of costs, taking account of a price limit established in the product's development phase. For a period of two years (three years for products introduced in 1984 and 1985) extra profits were allowed. All of these arrangements intended to increase the rewards enjoyed for introducing new innovations and products, and to discourage the continued production of goods approaching obsolescence.

In conjunction with the combine reform and the plan-perfecting measures, the rights of those institutions monitoring the performance of producers were extended; additionally, some new ones were created (e.g., the State Balancing Inspection, and Inspections for Quality). These new institutions contributed to the success of the first half of the 1980s as the consumption of energy and materials was considerably reduced in production processes and more efficient use of labour and capital were achieved. Inadequacies remained, however, with respect to the adoption of new innovation, the

---

[23] By 1986 a total of 1,135 balances were still generated by the central organs (of which 451 were by the state planning commission and 684 by the ministries). Balances prepared at the combine level had increased to 3,400, which can be interpreted as a modest reduction in the state's influence.

motivation of labour and other agents, and efficiency in general. In spite of the achieved improvements, the indirect steering mechanism emphasized negative incentives and undervalued positive ones. Production units still had few possibilities to utilize earnings for purposes of their own choosing.[24]

'All-Encompassing Intensification' in the Later 1980s

Planning for the 1986–1990 quinquennium started from the assumption that growth was to be based primarily upon technological progress and innovation.[25] 'All-encompassing intensification' (*umfassende Intensivierung*) refers to the complex, balanced use of intensive growth factors to achieve the greatest possible effect.[26] The objective was to economize on resources, while quickly channelling them into completely new production lines.[27] It was also considered very important to achieve a significant upgrading of commodities and production processes.[28]

East German economists pointed out the basic principles underlying the intensification campaign. Essential to its success was that new products should show a positive difference between 'value' and cost, so as to provide advantages for the user. Lasting impulses for innovation in products and production technologies were to come

---

[24] For more details see Manfred Melzer: 'The Perfecting of the Planning and Steering Mechanisms', in Ian Jeffries and Manfred Melzer (eds), *The East German Economy* (London: Croom Helm, 1987), pp. 99–118.

[25] See Harald Rost *et al.*, *Planungsordnung 1986–1990 – Wichtiges Instrument zur Verwirklichung der ökonomischen Strategie*, Reihe: Blickpunkt Wirtschaft, no. 3 (Berlin [East]: Verlag die Wirtschaft, 1985) p. 16.

[26] Siegfried Wenzel, 'Fragen der umfassenden Intensivierung in Auswertung der 9. Tagung des ZK der SED', *Effektivität der Volkswirtschaft in der intensiv erweiterten Reproduktion*, ed. Akademie der Wissenschaften der DDR, no. W3/1985, p. 17.

[27] Wolfgang Heinrichs, 'Umfassende Intensivierung und Reproduktionstheorie', *Wirtschaftswissenschaft*, vol. 32, no. 7 (1984) pp. 961ff.

[28] See Heinz Jurk, Gerhard Scholl, Werner Lauerwald, and Oswald Schindelarz, 'Durch höhere Veredlung zu einem kontinuierlichen Leistungsanstieg unserer Volkswirtschaft', *Höhere Veredlung – Grundlage für Leistungssteigerungen*, Reihe: Blickpunkt Wirtschaft, no. 2 (Berlin [East]: Verlag die Wirtschaft, 1985) pp. 8ff.

through progress in research and development.[29] Input savings were to be achieved through product and technology renewal; those already achieved through savings measures would likely be duplicated thereafter only under increasing difficulties and with concomitant losses elsewhere.[30] These principles undergirded the East German attempt to achieve optimal production results and cost-minimization, but there is a limit to what can be accomplished in an economy burdened with distorted, non-scarcity prices fixed by the state.

The problem confronting the GDR in the mid-1980s was that the planners continued to introduce additional monitoring and control measures (new norms) into an already complicated planning process. They attempted to overcome price distortions to make efficiency measurable, and to provide production units with more resources for badly needed investments. What was needed were real incentives for enterprise and combine managers to actually implement innovations. Simply permitting production units to use their own earnings would have been one straightforward means of achieving this objective. One should not wonder that the combines and enterprises showed little interest in achieving better quality and in implementing real (rather than phantom) innovations.

In the second half of the 1980s some modest but interesting plan-perfecting measures were introduced. It was apparent, however, that these measures did not represent a convincing strategy for the achievement of a high rate of product and process renewal. The main changes were as follows:

1. The combines, ministries, and regional organs were instructed to show how proposed innovations would fit into various intensification scenarios.[31] These agencies were thus to contribute to the realization of the concept of 'substantially upgraded production'.

---

[29] See Hans-Joachim Beyer, 'Zu den neuen Leistungsansprüchen umfassender Intensivierung' in *Effektivität der Volkswirtschaft, op. cit.*, p. 54ff.
[30] See Wolfgang Heinrichs, 'Effektivitätsdynamik in der umfassenden Intensivierung', in *Effektivität der Volkswirtschaft, op. cit.*, p. 47.
[31] See Gertraude Hummel, 'Die Veredelungskonzeption der Kombinate – Instrument zur Erhöhung der Effektivität der Produktion', in *Effektivität der Volkswirtschaft, op. cit.*, p. 54.

They were required to document in detail what they were doing to achieve product and process renewal, to develop new products and improve product quality, to implement new techniques, to modernize and rationalize production processes to continue cost savings efforts, and to perform other intensification tasks.

2. The centre undertook to link plan indicators to achieve 'efficiency planning'.[32] It was stipulated, for example, that the growth of labour productivity must exceed that of net production; that increases in labour productivity must exceed increases in wages and in capital per employee; and that exports of new commodities should increase faster than R&D expenditures.[33] Since existing prices were an inadequate measuring rod for efficiency (as was the 'realized profit' measure), GDR authorities hoped that increased efficiency might be stimulated and measured by these new indicators.

3. GDR authorities emphasized the development of 'key technologies'[34] in special long- and short-run plans. A substantial part of the M11.5 billion spent for science and technology was to flow into these sectors. Within those plans state orders played an increasing role; they were concentrated on structurally important projects (for 1986–90 the number was reported at forty).[35] Combine projects were to be kept under strict control through the use of appropriate instruments. All producers were to document their production results, along with anticipated earned revenues to be realized from R&D projects, in a 'Dossier of Duties'

---

[32] See Peter Hoss, 'Zur stärkeren Ausrichtung der volkswirtschaftlichen Rechnungsführung auf die Steigerung der Effektivität der gesellschaftlichen Produktion' in *Effektivität der Volkswirtschaft, op. cit.,* p. 90f.
[33] See Harald Rost *et al., Planungsordnung, op. cit.,* p. 3. Production units also had to show the economic effects of robots and microelectronic equipment in use, what savings of input had been achieved, and what effects the saved resources had on efficiency in other production.
[34] The reference here was to such fields as microelectronics, robots, CAD/CAM stations, computers, laser techniques, biotechniques, communications, etc.
[35] *Neues Deutschland,* 28 November 1986, p. 6.

(*Pflichtenheft*). The *Pflichtenheft* was also the required basis for the initiation and implementation of a research project. Expected costs and benefits of the proposed project had to be supported by a variety of technical data, e.g., production cost ceilings, foreign-currency profitability, etc.[36] Following the appearance of additional regulations in 1987, a so-called 'Renewals Passport' (*Erneuerungspass*) was to document these and additional items. This latter document was also to contain the DG's strategy for implementing proposed projects over the following two years.

With the issue of new regulations during 1986 and in the following year, closer cooperation was achieved between production units on the one side and the academy of sciences, universities and other research institutions on the other.[37] The production units were encouraged to finance more basic research, and the universities were to concentrate more on key technologies in order to provide concrete assistance for the production units and give them incentive to seek new solutions to production and technology problems. The desired cooperation in developing new technologies was to be realized on the basis of contracts.[38] The contractual aspect of these regulations is significant because when individual combines and enterprises can make their own arrangements in research and

---

[36] See 'Verordnung über den Erneuerungspass und das Pflichtenheft, *Gesetzblatt der DDR*, part I/1986, pp. 409ff.
[37] See 'Besschluß über Grunsätze für die Gestaltung ökonomischer Beziehungen der Kombinate der Industrie mit den Einrichtungen der Akademie der Wissenschaften sowie des Hochschulwesens', *Gesetzblatt der DDR*, part I/1986, pp 9ff, and 'Verordnung über die Leitung, Planung und Finanzierung der Forschung an der Akademie der Wissenschaften der DDR und an Univeritäten und Hochschulen, insbesondere der Forschungskooperation mit den Kombinaten', *Gesetzblatt der DDR*, part I/1986, pp. 12ff.
[38] For more detais see Angela Scherzinger, 'DDR: Instrumentarium für Forschung und Entwicklung ausgebaut', *Wochenbericht des DIW*, no. 19/1987. See also that author's 'Die Aufgaben der Hochschulen und der Akademie der Wissenschaften beim Wissens- und Technologietransfer in der DDR', *Vierteljahrshefte zur Wirtschaftsforschung des DIW*, no. 4/1987, pp. 309–20.

production, they are achieving the 'self-management' that is such an essential part of the general reform concepts currently prevalent in the Soviet Union and Eastern Europe. As is apparent in the East German case, this arrangement is taken for granted.

But traditional difficulties in the field of innovation remained. They were well expressed in the following, typical observation:[39] 'What good is dynamic development for the producer of a consumer good, when the producer of an important input either does not want to or cannot follow suit? What good is a new invention if the relevant industrial enterprise is actually unable to produce it?'

4. A revaluation of all fixed assets was accomplished in 1986, based on current capital goods prices.[40] In achieving that task, coefficients for some 300 different groups of fixed assets were used.[41] On average, the new values for all sectors were 30 per cent higher than those at 1980 prices. They were designed to provide an improved measure of profitability and capital productivity, since the revaluation based the capital charge on the net (rather than gross) value of fixed assets.[42] Along with the capital revaluation, new depreciation rates were established.[43]

---

[39] See Uwe Jens Heuer, 'Wirtschaftsdynamik und Recht', *Spectrum*, no. 10/1986, p. 1. For more on innovation problems see Kurt Erdmann, 'Innovationsbemühungen und zentrale Planung – Kernanliegen des Wirtschaftssystems der DDR', *FS-Analysen*, no. 5 (1986) pp. 5–58.

[40] See 'Anordnung über die Umbewertung der Grundmittel', *Gesetzblatt der DDR*, part I/1984, pp. 450–451. For more on the price changes see Kurt Erdmann: Verhaltene Änderungen in Kombinaten der DDR – Technikeinsatz und Experimente', *Glasnost und Perestroika auch in der DDR?* Berlin (West): Forschungsstelle für gesamtdeutsche wirtschaftliche und soziale Fragen (1988) pp. 141–150.

[41] See Arno Donda, 'Die Umbewertung der Grundmittel schafft reale Wertmaßstaebe', *Modernisierung – Hauptform der Grundfondsreproduktion*, Reihe: Blickpunkt Wirtschaft, no. 4 (Berlin [East]: Verlag die Wirtschaft, 1985) pp. 81ff.

[42] See 'Verordnung über die Produktionsfondsabgabe', *Gesetzblatt der DDR*, part I/1985, pp. 157–8.

[43] See 'Anordnung über die Abschreibungen der Grundmittel', *Sonderdruck des Gesetzblattes*, no. 1124 (1985).

These reform steps were incorporated into the Planning Order (*Ordnung der Planung*) for the Years 1986–1990, a document which states the principles and methods of plan implementation for the relevant five year period. Implemented in 1984 and 1985, these measures were intended to stabilize the entire planning process; nevertheless, a considerable number of changes proved necessary after that time. They took the form of supplemental orders or even of changes in whole sections of the planning order. All these changes demonstrated, at least, that East German planning improvement (later, 'reform') was in fact an ongoing process, even if change was not always readily observable from outside the GDR.

Let us consider some of the main changes of the Planning Order, since they reflect the previous regime's preferences for 'reform', and they could be starting point for more significant change to follow. They included the following:

1. A rapid growth of plan indicators. For the period 1986 to 1990, basically 156 indicators were given; but in 1986 and 1987 this number was increased to 172 and then to 214,[44] many of these being for production, foreign trade, and foreign currency relations. Indicators for energy savings and for the microelectronics sector were also introduced, although those on 'normal' rationalization were abandoned.

2. In the place of the partial plan for rationalization, a new one was introduced for the accelerated development and use of microelectronics, and CAD/CAM and computer techniques. For this 'special' rationalization process, centrally-guided production units were required to monitor around 55 plan indicators.[45]

---

[44] See the first three Decrees on 'Die Ordnung der Planung der Volkswirtschaft der DDR 1986 bis 1990, part A, *Gesetzblatt der DDR*, part I/1986, pp. 185ff, and Sonderdruck des Gesetzblattes der DDR, no. 1190a (1985) and no. 1190/1a (1987).

[45] See 'Planung der beschleunigten Entwicklung und Anwendung der Mikroelectronik, CAD/CAM-und Rechentechnik', in 'Anordnung Nr. 3 über die Ordnung der Planung der Volkwirtschaft der DDR 1986 bis 1990, part L. Sonderdruck des Gesetzblattes der DDR, no. 1190/11 (1987), pp. 5–27.

3. As we have seen, in the later years of the Honecker regime increasing importance was attached to efficiency and performance calculations based on a combination of plan indicators.[46] These measures ranked (a) growth indicators and (b) indicators pertaining to resource use and production costs. Coefficients thus established were related to other basic indicators, suggesting performance standards that might lead to the achievement of intensive growth. Examples: output growth was to exceed the increase of costs for each M100 worth of commodities produced; hard currency yields from the export of new products were to exceed the average yields of exports in general; the share of new commodities exported was to exceed the share of new commodities in total production. Such indicators were to help planners perceive, for example, what the contribution of plant renewal was to economic growth, what role R&D expenditures played either in the reduction of energy and materials use or in the expansion of exports, and what the effects of CAD/CAM solutions were on the performance of individual branches. All of these measures might in fact be interesting, but where incentive incompatibilities permeate an economic system, performance will remain poor regardless of the wide varieties of measurement to which it might be subjected.

4. In 1988 the Order of Planning introduced three changes in material balancing and planning[47] to be incorporated into the planning process for 1989. The objective was to incorporate the planning of materials use for product upgrading and new technologies more effectively into the total planning effort, in other words, to achieve better coordination. Material balancing, it was believed, needed to be expanded to account for special materials

---

[46] See 'Planung der Effektivität der gesellschaftlichen Produktion', in 'Anordnung Nr. 3 über Ordnung der Planung', *op. cit.*, pp. 97–111.
[47] See 'Anordnung Nr. 4 über die Ergänzung der Ordnung der Planung der Volkswirtschaft der DDR 1986 bis 1990', part M, *Sonderdruck des Gesetzblattes der DDR*, no. 1190/1m–I, 1m–II (1987), and 1m–III (1988).

and semi-finished parts required to produce key technologies, new products, goods of high export profitability, and consumer goods. For this purpose the preparation of five types of balance was required: (a) for energy use, (b) for materials and other inputs, (c) for equipment, (d) for consumer goods, and (e) for industrial plants in preparation. In order actually to acquire these balanced inputs, the *Kombinate* and enterprises were instructed to submit extensive amounts of documentation justifying their demands for inputs.

These activities certainly do not reflect any inclination to decentralize. But possibly even more important than the apparent increase in centralization were some other factors:

(a) With computerized operations the centre had gained the capacity to determine immediately the fields of performance in which some combines could reach high levels of efficiency, productivity, input savings, etc. Their analysis of performance through the available indicators enabled the state organs to locate bottlenecks and initiate action to overcome problems quickly.

(b) The center was trying to achieve certain structural changes in production to achieve better implementation of key technologies, more effective use of those already in place, and a more rapid upgrading of products. But the pronounced scarcity of inputs, especially in areas where such improvements were sought, made it necessary to refine the system of allocation and the monitoring of the resources used.

It was impossible for the 1989 plan to achieve consistency in all of the material balances. Refinements in balancing processes could more readily illuminate the specific location of crucial input shortages than overcome them. Guenter Mittag, Honecker's chief economic strategist insisted that the combines should develop the ability to produce their own quality inputs,[48] but that could not have

---

[48] See Guenter Mittag, 'Einheit von Wirtschafts– und Sozialpolitik ist das Kernstück unserer Gesellschaftskonzeption', *Neues Deutschland*, 13 March, 1987, p. 3.

been the answer to this problem. Taken as a *reductio ad absurdum*, the suggestion calls for the rejection of division of labour in industry, reducing, in effect, all the coefficients of an input-output table of the GDR economy to zero.

THE EXPERIMENTAL KOMBINATE

The weaknesses of socialist economic mechanisms are well known; they include widespread sluggishness in innovation, weak managerial and labour motivation, insufficient competitive forces, and a rather rigid, noncompetitive supply structure. These flaws are compounded by scarcity in energy, materials, investment, and consumer goods supplies, distorted price structures, and so on. All these inadequacies suggested the urgency of effective reform steps. Plan 'perfecting' had accomplished a number of things, but had not overcome such fundamental insufficiencies as the chronic tardiness of new investment projects and the inadequacies of supply (in terms of quantity and quality) of raw materials and intermediate inputs.

Some progress was made when the GDR introduced in late 1986 the 'full use' of the principle of enterprise 'internal resource generation' (*Eigenerwirtschaftung der Mittel*). According to this principle, production units should not only cover current expenditures from their own revenues, but also (apart from some budgetary grants in special cases) finance investment from profits, depreciation allowances, and interest-bearing credits. This innovation demonstrated the party's high priority on the achievement of more efficient investment and more rapid implementation of innovations,[49] reflecting the party's very healthy interest in returning a greater degree of economic independence to the individual enterprises within the combines,

---

[49] See Guenter Mittag, 'Leitung, Planung und wirtschaftliche Rechnungsführung in der Volkswirtschaft der DDR', *Einheit*, no. 10 (1986) p. 881.

or creating greater self-management where it had not previously
existed.

Here was an opportunity to move away from some of the weaknesses inherent in the centralist characteristics of the combine
system.[50] The need was great. First, immense disproportions between centrally and regionally directed combines were still extant.
Second, there were great differences in the performance levels of the
individual combines: this is partly because some DGs saw themselves
merely as executors of state policy, while others thought of themselves as entrepreneurs and performed as such. Third, there were
still significant problems within the combines, since the position
of the enterprise managers did not vouchsafe significant decision
prerogatives or significant influence on combine policy. For this, of
course, the combine directors were largely responsible. Observing
this problem, Honecker cautiously pointed out in February 1988,
that 'we certainly must pay attention to the question of enterprise
independence within the *Kombinate*'.[51]

There was movement away from the centralization of revenue use
by the combine's Director General. Enterprises were encouraged
to pursue 'internal resource generation', with an explicit intent to
enhance the role of profitability for the enterprise. Nevertheless,
the DG remained legally empowered to reassign production tasks,
equipment, and funds between enterprises and/or to the parent
enterprise. That policy was, of course, in opposition to the belated
socialist conviction that enterprises can be motivated properly only
when they can retain for their own purposes a substantive portion of
the fruits of their accomplishments.

Some new ideas were introduced in a less experimental manner

---

[50] See Phillip J. Bryson, 'East German Traditional Centralism: An Alternative
Route to Economic Reconstruction', *The Annals of the American Academy
of Political and Social Science*, vol. 507 (January 1990) pp. 133–141, and
Manfred Melzer, 'Die Rolle der Kombinate und Betriebe im Wirtschafts-
system der DDR, In Hans-Erich Gramatzki and Hans G. Nutzinger, eds.,
Betrieb und Partizipation in Osteuropa (Frankfurt and New York: Campus
Verlag, 1986) pp. 445–70.
[51] Erich Honecker, 'Mit dem Volk und Für das Volk', *op. cit.*, p. 16.

in all combines and enterprises. The new investment fund was an example:[52] for the combine or for an individual enterprise, it was to be formed from amortization (40 per cent) and retained earnings (60 per cent);[53] from this source, up to five million Marks could be invested at the discretion of the fund's steward. In the case of the enterprise, the DG had to approve of the allocation; but it is important that the enterprise fund could not be accessed by the DG.[54] To implement projects of this type, the enterprises still had to produce for themselves the equipment they needed for the project. If opportunities for the effective expenditure of retained earnings had actually existed (investment equipment had actually been available for purchase), greater efficiency could have been achieved as enterprises attempted to improve productivity, reduce costs, introduce innovations, and so on, in the pursuit of profitable performance.

Because of the inherent risks associated with the implementation of some new policies, however, GDR economic authorities began implementing these only in a limited number of combines. The program introduced in the experimental *Kombinate* in 1988 was to test some new incentives, especially those providing production units with discretionary use of incremental profits.[55] The primary objective was to reduce bureaucracy while enhancing the role of profit and making production units more independent. Planners hoped to permit the enterprises greater freedom in some investment decisions while retaining the advantages of planning the development of certain

---

[52] 'Anordnung über die Planung, Bildung und Verwendung des eigenverantwortlich zu erwirtschaftenden und zu verwendenden Investitionsfonds', *Gesetzblatt der DDR*, part I/1987, pp. 15–18.
[53] See Karl-Heinz Arnold, 'Guter Gewinn als Basis eigener Investitionen Erweitete Verantwortung für Kombinate und Betriebe', *Berliner Zeitung*, 3 March 1987, p. 3.
[54] To account for the new investment fund, the previously extant 'performance fund' was appropriately altered. Up to 1987, the means of rationalization could be financed. This was removed from the regulations since those means of rationalization were later to be financed from the new investment fund. See 'Anordnung über den Leistungsfonds zur Verbesserung der Arbeits- und Lebensbedingungen, *Gesetzblatt der DDR*, part I/1987, pp. 18, 19.
[55] See *Tribüne*, 18 January 1989, p. 2.

industrial structures. Important measures included the following:

– In connection with a planned reduction in the number of centrally directed investment projects, some discussion was devoted to reducing the number of plan indicators.

– The production units were allowed to keep a greater share of earned profits.

– There was a plan to keep some norms in effect for more than a single year; a certain part of extra profit might be saved, for example, for use in a future period.

– On an experimental basis, the production fund levy was to be financed out of costs rather than from profits.

– Production units were permitted to retain a certain and increasing share of foreign currency earnings. These were to be used to import technologies and spare parts.

– The fund for science and technology was no longer to be financed out of costs, but out of profit in order to encourage the combines and enterprises to save funds used for R&D.

– General repairs were to be financed from amortization funds rather than being seen as 'costs' to be financed from the repairs fund, taking into account that general repairs increase the value and the life of capital goods.

– To better motivate the labour force, consideration was given to relating the wage fund to labour productivity.

Changes along these lines were undertaken in a similar way in all the sixteen experimental combines, so that they came to function with much greater independence than the rest of the economy's producers. It had originally been foreseen for the experiment to be expanded to fifty-two industrial and construction combines in 1989,[56] and it was hoped that even more would be involved in 1990, so that the next five-year plan could begin on the basis of these improvements in the economy as a whole. After all, the performance of the sixteen experimental combines in 1988 was much better than that of the other combines in industry: an increase in labour productivity reached 10.6 per cent (compared with 7.0) and a reduction in costs of 1.8 per cent (compared with 1.0).[57] Therefore, General Secretary Honecker and economic strategist Guenter Mittag had praised the full use of the principle of enterprise 'internal resource generation'.[58]

In the investment sector a complicated situation arose. Apart from the most important centrally determined investment projects (about three hundred), two other project types could be instigated through self-management decisions at the level of the production units. These decentralized project types were (a) limited projects of up to M5 million in value for producers who were not included in the sixteen or more experimenting combines, and (b) projects of unlimited size for producers who were included in the elite sixteen. The large projects of this type were designed to enhance the possibilities of the experimenting combines in their pursuit of profit and to permit them to utilize a greater variety of possibilities for financing investments.

A fourth investment category included those which were neither of the above-mentioned self-management units nor a part of the state plan. This consisted of investments of a value in excess of M5 million undertaken by combines still subject to the regulations of 1987 (not yet subject to the principles of self-management).[59] The size of this latter project type was determined by the centre; such projects were to be prepared by the state planning committee and financed through enterprise funds or by credits from the state budget. The intention was to continue pursuing centrally prepared projects, but also to move toward self-determined projects of even very large scale.

---

[57] See Harald Rost, 'Was ist der Kern des Prinzips der Eigenerwirtschaftung der Mittel?' *Bauern-Echo*, 17 May 1989, p. 5.

[58] See Erich Honecker, 'Mit dem Blick auf den XII Parteitag die Aufgaben der Gegenwart lösen (Aus dem Bericht des Politbüros an die 7. Tagung des ZK der SED)', *Neues Deutschland*, 2 December 1988, pp. 6/7. See also Guenter Mittag, 'Hohe Leistungen aller Kombinate auf dem Weg zum XII Parteitag', *Neues Deutschland*, 9 March 1989, p. 5.

[59] See 'Anordnung no. 5 über die Ergänzung der Ordnung der Planung der Volkswirtschaft der DDR 1986 bis 1990 vom 16. Januar 1989', *Sonderdruck des Gesetzblattes der DDR*, no. 1190/21, 'Planung der Grundfonds und Investitionen', pp. 5–16.

There was no apparent intent on the part of the centre to relinquish its influence at the stage of investment preparations. This preliminary phase remained subject to the traditional regulatory powers of the planners as they monitored capacity utilization in the industry, enforced efficiency criteria, checked for conformity to science and technology regulations, and so on. The implementation of investment projects continued to subject investing firms to the direction of the state planning commission, which in cases of enterprise infractions was required to 'remove insufficiencies immediately with an on-the-spot evaluation of the corrective measures'.[60] Banks were to play an increased role in monitoring these investments,[61] and they were to enjoy more active credit policy, including the right to intervene in cases where they concluded that planned profitability could not be achieved.[62]

All of this seemed to ignore the newly-won decision prerogatives of GDR production units. It is quite apparent that GDR economic leadership found it exceedingly difficult to overcome the tendency to over-manage the activities of production agents. When greater room for manoeuvring was granted to such agents, the situation had first to be carefully monitored, then hedged around with new regulations. As is evident from the history of these last years of the Honecker regime, the hostility to reform was combined with instincts and actions that would have subverted any genuine attempt to achieve economic renewal. The covert possibilities for reform inherent in the halting, self-management experiments in the sixteen or more combines could serve after the cataclysm only as the most modest beginnings of genuine reform.

Honecker pointed out that from 1981 to 1985, 40 per cent of the increase in national income was the result of reduced input requirements. In 1987 the reduction amounted only to 29 per cent,

---

[60] See 'Verordnung über die Vorbereitung und Durchführung von Investitionen vom 30. November 1988', *Gesetzblatt der DDR*, Teil I/1988, pp. 287ff.

[61] Cf. 'Dritte Verordnung über die Kreditgewährung und die Bankkontrolle der sozialistischen Wirtschaft vom 30. November 1988', *Gesetzblatt der DDR*, Teil I/1988, pp. 283ff.

[62] See *Berliner Zeitung*, 10 January 1989, p. 3.

and Honecker demanded a reversal of the tendency.[63] The plan was to install successful changes implemented in the experimental combines through all industries by 1991. But in June 1989, politburo member Joachim Herrmann announced that the plan to expand the number of experimental combines to forty would be postponed to 1990.[64] In doing so, he emphasized that self-management in the pursuit of the intensification is a worthy objective but it does not diminish the responsibility for the achievement of plan targets. In the balance between the plan and self-management, Hermann didn't want the plan forgotten.

This postponement left the sixteen combines as a sort of island in the midst of a sea of direct planning. Their relations with the rest of the economy were more difficult as a result of the differences, which tended to encourage them to expand the economic exchange of goods and materials among their own number.

INTERIM CONCLUSIONS

In the wake of the cataclysm three approaches to economic regeneration gradually became apparent. The first attempt was what intellectuals in and beyond the GDR anticipated: interim and post-election regimes would attempt to introduce reform gradually. Even the gradualist approach would suggest that implementation of the experimental self-management principles (or of greater changes) would be tried very early. It was not clear that such change would have a uniformly significant impact on all combines, given their widely divergent general performance and productive efficiency levels. Some combines scarcely had a technical programme, and in some enterprises the standard of economic accounting was not very high. But it was clear that some combines would be dismantled in order to give their member enterprises more room for manoeuvre.

The second possible approach would involve a new era of genuine

---

[63] Erich Honecker, Mit dem Volk und für das Volk', *op. cit.*, p. 34.
[64] See Joachim Herrmann, 'Aus dem Bericht des Politbüros an die 8. Tagung des ZK der SED', *Neues Deutschland*, 23 June 1989, p. 3.

reform, which would cause nearly all of the traditional hierarchical steps discussed above to be scrapped for more significant decentralization efforts and a more market-oriented approach. Those traditional plan improving measures just reviewed were much more conservative than East Germans demanded after the collapse of the Honecker era. Nevertheless, it was to be expected that there would be a significant inertia in GDR society as a result of the strong residual effects of earlier socialist indoctrination, and the legacy of socialist economics in the academic establishment. Remnants of the Honecker regime would have a preference for retaining the traditional elements of a centrally planned economy.

But after the cataclysm public pressure did not permit the dominance of party and planning to prevail. East Germans did not yet have a good perception of alternatives to socialist economics, but immediately to the west there was a plethora of ideas on how to reconstruct. The third approach, the coming of which was rather breathtaking for the long-time observer of East German socialism, was that of economic union with the Federal Republic. It is amazing how rapidly reactionary socialist forces crumbled before the perception of economic deterioration associated with the continuing emigration beyond the *Wende*. Only a brief three months after the removal of Honecker, *de facto* economic reunification[65] appeared unstoppable, formal economic union not far away[66] – and who would then have prophesied that complete unification would be achieved by 3 October, 1990? We will return to these developments in Chapter 4.

It is important to observe, however, that before the cataclysm the GDR economy was not an island of socialism, but an integral

---

[65] The interest of West Germans in investment possibilities in the GDR and the growing desire of East Germans to achieve the economic security promised *only* by West Germany were significant impressions from the first few weeks after the cataclysm. Western observers felt that the private flow of capital to East Germany would of itself amount to a *de facto* form of reunification.

[66] Formal reunification was suggested as a possible response very early, as was the adoption of the West German DM as the common currency of both Germanies at a very early point.

part of the community of socialist nations of East Europe. The challenges emanating from the external environment, the demands of international trade and integration of that period (not to mention those associated with the more substantial levels of activity all the socialist countries longed for) augmented the domestic and international political pressures for change in a powerful way. We turn in Chapter 3 to a consideration of the complexities the GDR economy encountered in interacting with the socialist and world markets.

3   The GDR in the International Economy

With the Soviet Union and other East European countries officially bent on implementing Gorbachev's 'radical and revolutionary' reform, the GDR was under considerable pressure to do more than merely persist with 'plan perfecting'. But this chapter addresses another form of pressure that augmented and intensified the political pressure favouring economic change and a more open system. This additional and (in the long term perhaps even more) compelling pressure emanated from the manifest need of an advanced economy to be an active player in world markets. Modern economies simply must be integrated into the worldwide system of international specialization and division of labour. Economic change emanating from the Soviet Union, the most significant trading partner of the GDR, from the Council for Mutual Economic Assistance (CMEA), from the Federal Republic of Germany (FRG), and from the European Community (EC), would ultimately have had an impact upon the East German economy similar to what we have observed from domestic political pressure.

As a result of earlier reform developments in Eastern Europe, traditional foreign economic relationships became more uncertain toward the end of the Honecker years. This section will address the complex of international economic questions which, given the GDR's trade dependence,[1] was preoccupying many of Berlin's best minds after about 1987.

---

[1]   In 1986 East German trade turnover, exports plus imports (= 181.9 billion Valuta Marks) represented (if one overlooks an apples–oranges comparison to conceptualize the rough relative magnitudes) .722 of that year's produced national income (252.2 billion Marks). See the *Statistisches Taschenbuch der Deutschen Demokratischen Republik, 1988* (Berlin [East]: Staatsverlag der Deutschen Demokratischen Republik, 1988).

A tentative strategy had, in fact, been developed under the old regime, and GDR economic and planning specialists were actively engaged in its articulation and refinement. As we shall have cause to observe below, a key element of that strategy was authorizing industrial combines and enterprises to make their own foreign trade decisions, including the establishment of direct inter-firm relationships (DIFR) between production units. It may be that the progress of economic reform or decentralization can best be measured by the progress a reforming country makes in decontrolling the international activities of its producers. Such progress has always been difficult to achieve in countries that grew up believing the state's foreign trade monopoly should make decisions in the interests of society as a whole. To a limited extent (as we shall explain below), the GDR's economics establishment shared this desire with other socialist countries.

In the first section we will consider the GDR's endeavour to manage *domestic* economic activity so as to achieve an effective international economic performance – one which would also be politically and socially acceptable. We will consider in the second section the basic foreign trade and integration strategy, while the third section will address GDR trade and integration policies toward the Soviet Union and the CMEA. Finally, a fourth section will conclude with a discussion of the GDR's strategy toward the Federal Republic of Germany and other Western trading partners.

KEY DOMESTIC ELEMENTS OF INTERNATIONAL PLANNING

It would be senseless, of course, to pursue a reform of international economic institutions while ignoring characteristics of the domestic economy which would prohibit effective international performance. Honecker's strategists recognized that adaptation to the external environment would require adjustments in the organization of the domestic economy. They did not fail to see the central significance in this regard of achieving enterprise self-management (*Eigenerwirtschaftung*).

Enterprise Autonomy

The GDR's planning improvement measures had already expanded the decision prerogatives of the combine's director general (DG). Directly prior to the cataclysm, these prerogatives were especially apparent in the area of investments, as was emphasized in Chapter 2. It is of significance that the latest strategy of the Honecker regime would ultimately have left central planners responsibility only for producers' *long-run success*; the theory was that they would be denied intervention in enterprise daily affairs. It was hoped that the central organs would generally limit their activities to structural questions.

In actual practice, GDR micro-industrial organization was far from embracing enterprise self-management. In too many industries, devolution did not really extend beyond the DG, and the managers of too many enterprises gained precious little autonomy. Thus, Becker and Ebersbach, two east German economists, could say no more about enterprise autonomy than that there had been some experimentation in expanding it. Permitting combines to submit suggestions for the resolution of economic and technical cooperation problems (especially in production and research specialization), and allowing foreign trade enterprises to participate in the preparation and coordination of the five-year plans had 'worked out well' in practice.[2] These authors observed that combines achieved better market flexibility and response in international markets when the component enterprises helped delineate the combine's overall strategy, and likewise when they were permitted to develop their own individual strategy.[3]

The attempt was already being made before the *Wende* to prepare combines to participate more freely and directly in the enhancement of the socialist international division of labour in science, technology, and production. This was to be achieved through

---

2   Cf. E. Becker and A. Ebersbach, 'Zu neuen Leitungsanforderungen an die langfristig-konzeptionelle Arbeit der Kombinate bei der weiteren Vertiefung der Zusammenarbeit mit den RGW-Partnern', *Wirtschaftswissenschaft*, 37, no. 3 (1989) pp. 388.
3   Ibid., p. 393.

'the development of direct relations (*Direktbeziehungen*) between socialist enterprises, both domestically and internationally'.[4] The East German discussion on direct inter-firm relations (DIFR) was quite positive about pursuing the idea, but concluded that it would be some time before such relations could be achieved. The DIFR theme will be addressed at length later; let it suffice here to note that the actual achievement of such relations would have required enterprise and combine autonomy in the use of earned foreign receipts of convertible currencies.[5]

Pursuing Optimal Centralization in Foreign Trade and Integration

Having recognized that excessive centralization of foreign activities was destructive of incentives and of flexible response to changing market conditions, the GDR intended to move away from direct controls.[6] Nevertheless, the conviction remained evident that the overall economy must continue to be organised under central leadership. Otherwise, narrow enterprise or combine interests might supercede social interests, an outcome considered potentially damaging under enterprise self-financing. Likewise, the share of total output to be exported (that is, the share remaining

---

[4] See H. Koziolek (ed.), *Sozialistische ökonomische Integration und wissenschaftlich-technischer Fortschritt*, Abhandlungen der Akademie der Wissenschaften der DDR. Veröffentlichung der Wissenschaftlichen Räte (Berlin [East]: Akademie-Verlag, 1988) p. 7.

[5] See H.-J. Dubrowsky, 'Aspekte der Konvertierbarkeit sozialistischer Währungen', *Wirtschaftswissenschaft*, 37, no. 5 (1989) pp. 712–34, which was viewed by a number of GDR scholars as being the definitive statement on the issue of convertibility of socialist (especially GDR) currency. As Dubrowsky's italics emphasize: 'At the heart of the matter, the introduction of convertibility of the socialist currencies is the transferral to the economic units of the right to arrange their own foreign monetary relationships independently' (p. 726).

[6] According to Dubrowsky, *op. cit.*, p. 726, '*We do not face the alternative: central management and planning or independence, plan or market. Rather, success depends in every period of social development on finding the correct relationship, the optimal connection, between them.*' (His emphasis.)

for domestic consumption and development) would properly be decided at the centre, according to the prevailing view.[7]

In the last days of the Honecker era, there seemed to be a consensus among GDR economists that decisions to develop *inter alia* raw materials capacities, energy sources, and especially key technologies must be made at the centre in the interests of the economy as a whole. Koziolek, a leading economic strategist, held that the processes of technology development, like those of restructuring industries, are long-term ones requiring central direction. His categorical statement that markets 'do not perform those tasks' is not untrue. It merely blurs the fact that markets can and do play a role even in these allocation processes, the effectiveness of which sometimes depends on the degree to which competitive forces can be evoked.

Koziolek and Reinhold argued that R&D programmes increasingly require resources beyond those even of very large concerns. Such programmes are 'financed and organized by the state' in all highly developed industrial capitalist systems, and the centre must play that role in the GDR.[8] To the East German way of thinking, if firms can export, form joint ventures, and function in all areas with complete independence, the central direction of high technologies cannot be effective. This logic recommends retaining state ownership for the purposes of technology guidance.

The advantage of public ownership is also reflected in other important matters. Control over social property is viewed as facilitative of the imposition of central directives, primarily because managers are more amenable to social direction under state ownership than they would be under, say, capitalist indicative planning. In the latter case, suggestions from the centre may safely be regarded as of little concern to a private manager.

---

[7] As will become evident below, the GDR viewed the Soviet external reforms as ill-conceived, since hasty and excessive self-determination of Soviet enterprises regarding exports endangered not only standing inter-governmental delivery agreements, but also caused a drain of important inputs from the central supply system of Soviet Industry.

[8] See H. Koziolek and O. Reinhold, 'Plan und Markt im System unserer sozialistischen Planwirtschaft', *Einheit*, 44, no. 1 (1989) p. 18.

Luft[9] asserts that the most favourable proportionalities and efficiency derivable from foreign economic relations can *not* be realized by increasing decision prerogatives for individually isolated economic units, especially in a regime of spontaneous market relations. Enterprise responsibility on the one hand and central direction on the other were, for East Germans, not at all contradictory in international economic affairs. The economic plan was an irreplaceable prerequisite assuring the interests of the combines as they performed their activities more effectively and responded to long-term norms and other framework conditions designed in the social interest.

Although a nice balance was expressed between centralism and managerial independence, the practice under Honecker remained strongly biased toward central intervention. As the West German economist Hamel has observed, GDR leadership took pride in the timely resolution of its credit crisis in the early 1980s. But that was accomplished largely by a drastic reduction of imports, and by reducing the level of investments. This experience of the early 1980s might be taken as evidence that the political leadership was effectively able to concentrate its energies and resources on top priorities. Hamel concluded, therefore, that the central apparatus would not permit its monopoly powers in the foreign economic realm to be dismantled by reform experiments.[10]

That, of course, was under the *ancien regime*. After the turning point, the economic establishment was not immediately free of the bias imposed by the monolithic political system. Economists instincts were, doubtless, not all dismantled with the old government, although things can be seen differently in a pluralistic system. After the turning point, the relentless pressure of demonstrations and emigration produced substantive change in their pronouncements.

---

[9] Christa Luft, 'Entwicklungstendenzen bei der Leitung und Organisation der Außenwirtschaft in den RGW-Ländern und Schlußfolgerungen für ihre Zusammenarbeit', Helmut Koziolek (ed.), *Sozialistische ökonomische Integration und wissenschaftlich-technischer Fortschritt* (Berlin [East]: Akademie-Verlag, 1988) pp. 52–4. See especially p. 54.

[10] H. Hamel, 'Die DDR-Wirtschaft auf dem Weg zum "Entwickelten Sozialismus"' in *Wirtschaftsreformen im Ostblock in den 80er Jahren*, (ed.) R. Schlueter (Paderborn: Ferdinand Schoening, 1988) p. 76.

The 'reform' administration gradually found new views and heard new council from the country's economists.

Pricing

The achievement of reform in price formation processes is of key significance. If the necessary efficiency and incentives were to be achieved, distorted price relations had to be overcome; both the resolution of domestic economic problems and the achievement of effective interaction in world markets hinged on such pricing. This general proposition has been discussed extensively and needs no restatement here. If the East German economy had remained a captive implement of social policy (through the massive provision of subsidies for unrealistically and inefficiently low priced necessaries), it would have been impossible to adopt (necessarily higher) scarcity prices. It would also have remained impossible for GDR authorities to open their economy to give foreign buyers access to underpriced East German products. Foreign trade would also have had to be conducted essentially on a barter (negotiated rather than financial) basis, and convertibility could not have been achieved. By the same token, the CMEA countries will not achieve substantive trade and integration improvements until their respective pricing systems are reciprocally harmonized; achieving scarcity (generally, 'market') prices is the only way this can be done practically and continuously.

Even under Honecker it was difficult to find a professional economist who would argue against the necessity of achieving realistic prices. Most, however, seemed sympathetic to the political authorities, who never acquired the courage even to begin the price reform process by reducing subsidies and raising prices. Some of them, however, also pointed out that East Germans were gradually becoming conditioned to higher prices through their purchases in special shops (*Delikatläden*) in which higher quality goods were more expensive. Some of these items were also being sold in normal retail outlets at the higher prices. Additionally, substantially higher prices (functioning much like a tax to help defray the subsidy on necessaries) were attached to non-necessaries and durable goods. Such prices may have helped prepare East German buyers and

policymakers for the introduction of genuine prices. Until socialism produces a serious answer to its pricing problems, neither the
model of Soviet perestroika nor GDR *Planvervollkommnung* can be
considered worthy of the rubric 'economic reform'.

BASIC FOREIGN TRADE AND INTEGRATION STRATEGY

In the last years of the Honecker regime, the GDR found itself in a
rapidly changing external world. It was not clear whether the CMEA
countries would complete their economic reforms, whether socialist
economic integration would proceed, whether the EC would grow
further apart from the CMEA or develop mechanisms to include
East Europe, or whether the challenges associated with GDR
competitiveness in world markets would remain. Clearly, it was
essential for the GDR to exploit the growth opportunities foreign
trade offers. To do so, the GDR had to produce attractive, high
quality commodities, flexibly responding to demands in international markets.[11] Many East German economists believed this would
require that the GDR continue its attempt to develop key technologies (*Schlüsseltechnologien*), emphasizing the traditional German
strength in machine tool industries. Yet this strategy's continuing
lack of success in penetrating world markets was apparent.

The growth possibilities of foreign trade have been vividly demonstrated in recent years by the newly industrialized countries.
Nearly 25 per cent of all goods entering international trade origi-
nated from the Asian-Pacific region in 1985. Two decades previous
to that, that region's share had been only 10 per cent.[12] In the

---

[11] For an excellent review of the general objectives, institutions, and development of GDR foreign economic relations, see H.-H. Derix, and M. Haendcke-
Hoppe, 'Die Außenwirtschaftssysteme', *Materialien zum Bericht zur Lage
der Nation im geteilten Deutschland 1987*, Bundesministerium für inner-
deutsche Beziehungen, Bonn (1987) pp. 205–19.
[12] See A. Schüller, 'Zunehmende Internationalisierung der Wirtschaftsprozesse: Die DDR unter Anpassungsdruck', *Die Wirtschaftspolitik der Ära
Honecker – ökonomische und soziale Auswirkungen*, Teil 1, 14. Symposion
der Forschungsstelle am 17. und 18. November 1988, *FS Analysen*, no. 1
(1989), p. 14.

meantime, the GDR experienced a trend of slightly declining trade with the West, beginning from an already unsatisfactory level of activity. In 1988, while real import demand in the West was expanding by 8 per cent, the GDR could not profit from the mini-boom.[13]

To make matters worse, the GDR faced the necessity of making significant adjustments in its trade practices with the Soviet Union and other CMEA countries. Those previously comfortable sellers markets were undergoing challenging transformations, and conducting business with countries engaged in reform required many creative changes. Moreover, at the *Wende*, a larger share of East German trade was conducted by combines and enterprises new to that responsibility and experience.[14]

Under Honecker, the economic establishment sought to maintain a 'disturbance free' economy, avoiding or offsetting external disturbance. Continual reference was made to COCOM lists and credit blockades. In actual fact, some rather well known and very important disturbances came from the CMEA bloc itself, especially with regard to the delivery of energy. Collier indicates that a noteworthy reduction in the 1982 growth rate of East Germany's Net Material Product was the result of an approximate 7 per cent reduction by the Soviet Union in promised petroleum deliveries. This occurred 'literally without notice'. To make matters worse, Polish coal deliveries in 1982 'had fallen about 40 per cent below the level of 1980. The GDR's continued reliance on lignite becomes less puzzling in this light'.[15]

Another primary objective of the *ancien regime* was to try to remain (on the basis of its relative economic and technical strength within CMEA) the leading trade partner of the USSR.

---

[13] See Cornelsen, *op. cit.*, p. 59.
[14] See S. Möke, 'Das RGW-Komplexprogramm des wissenschaftlich-technischen Fortschritts und Fragen der weiteren Ausgestaltung des Systems der Zusammenarbeit der RGW-Länder', Helmut Kosiolek (ed.), *Sozialistische Ökonomische Integration und wissenschaftlich-technischer Fortschritt* (Berlin [East]: Akademie-Verlag, 1988) p. 36.
[15] See I. Collier, 'The GDR Five-Year Plan 1986–1990', in 'Symposium on the German Democratic Republic', Irwin Collier (ed.), *Comparative Economic Studies*, 29, no. 2 (Summer 1987), p. 40.

But GDR strategists had become very concerned that the Soviet Union might shift the locus of its trade and integration pattern to western countries. Improving its competitive position in Soviet trade had become as important as improving it in world markets. It was sensible, therefore, for the GDR to advertize its technical achievements, especially in microelectronics, and to demand that the CMEA define exclusive production specialties (with agreements to abstain from developing parallel production capacities).[16]

The hope that the CMEA would remain organizationally intact and that the GDR would continue to play a leading role in it did not imply any firm expectation that the CMEA would remain static or that life would remain largely as it had been. Observing the determination of trading partners to increase enterprise independence, achieve more effective DIFR, and establish joint enterprises (*gemeinsame Betriebe*), the GDR was attempting before the rebellion to convince the brother countries that this should occur in an environment of planned economic development and on a contractual basis.[17]

To pursue this strategy, the GDR was in the process of implementing the economic experimentation programme discussed in Chapter 2. In the sixteen participating combines, the centre hoped on the one hand, to retain the supposed advantages of central direction in developing priority industrial structures, while on the other hand increasing the independence of the selected production units. Along with the increased investment independence discussed previously, participants were permitted to retain a share of their foreign currency earnings for the purpose of acquiring imports of technology-laden equipment and spare parts.

---

[16] A skillful expositor and critic of this strategy was A. Schüller, 'Zunehmende Internationalisierung der Wirtschaftsprozesse: Die DDR unter Anpassungsdruck', *Die Wirtschaftspolitik der Ära Honecker – ökonomische und soziale Auswirkungen*, Teil 1, 14. Symposion der Forschungsstelle am 17. und 18. November 1988, *FS Analysen*, no. 1 (1989) pp. 11–13.

[17] Ibid., p. 23.

TRADE AND INTEGRATION WITH THE SOCIALIST COUNTRIES

Perhaps to its misfortune, the GDR had become considerably less dependent upon the ideological position of the Soviet Union toward the end of the Honecker era. But the leadership had not lost sight of East Germany's continued heavy dependence upon the USSR for raw materials[18] and as a central trading partner.[19]

Cooperation with the Soviet Union

Given the desire to nurture the critically important Soviet market, the East Germans had reason for concern about the impact of Soviet reforms on raw materials deliveries. For East German tastes, the Soviets too quickly dismantled their central supply system in pursuit of enterprise independence. The Germans observed that Soviet producers had sometimes exported scarce, domestically produced inputs (often, at prices that seemed too low), exacerbating shortages in Soviet industry. They expressed concern that the guaranteed, long-term raw materials and energy contracts concluded with the fraternal socialist government would gradually be phased out. Hence their insistence that the traditional methods of five year plan coordination should be preserved[20] in the area of energy trade.

The GDR had heavy commodity delivery obligations to the USSR to meet contracts for the financing of investments to tap soviet

---

[18] The 'reliable deliveries' of the USSR, during 1986–90, were scheduled to reach the following quantities: oil, 85.4 million tons; natural gas, 36 million cubic metres; refined steel, 16 million tons; cotton, 425,000 tons'. See M. Engert, 'Kampfgemeinschaft – Zusammenarbeit – sozialistische Integration', in *Sozialismus in der DDR: Gesellschaftsstrategie mit dem Blick auf das Jahr 2000* (Berlin [East]: Dietz Verlag, 1988) p. 188.

[19] Engert (ibid., p. 185) indicates that in billion Valuta-Marks the foreign trade turnover with the Soviet Union from 1971–75 was 99, from 1976–80 was 177, from 1981–85 was 303, and from 1986–90 was 380.

[20] Andreas Forner, 'Neue Aspekte der Fünfjahrplankoordinierung und Rolle des wissenschaftlich-technischen Fortschritts', Helmut Koziolek (ed.), *Sozialistische ökonomische Integration und wissenschaftlich-technischer Fortschritt* (Berlin [East]: Akademie-Verlag, 1988) p. 68.

energy and raw materials sources. It is not known what kind of pressures were put on the GDR and other CMEA countries to participate in these investments, but it is known that the Soviet/East bloc oil price in transferable rubles for 1986 and 1987 was almost twice as high as prices on world markets.[21]

To the extent that some GDR exports might be marketable in the West, the existing commodity delivery obligations to the Soviets were a burden on the ability of the GDR to service debt to western countries. But since East Germany would have liked to be able to use its limited foreign exchange earnings for badly needed investment equipment purchased in the West (rather than for energy and raw materials), it had to accept these investments in Soviet raw materials and energy.

Honecker era exports to the Soviet Union consisted mostly of final goods, especially of machinery and equipment[22] and consumer goods, largely textiles. The capacity to deliver such goods seemed to weaken somewhat over the last two or three years of the Honecker era, while the importation of Soviet goods increased in value terms by more than ten per cent, resulting in an unplanned, record deficit for the GDR of 750 million transferable rubles (TR) in 1986.[23] The deficit declined significantly thereafter. By 1986 the Soviets began to reject goods (*e.g.*, textiles) of insufficient quality, and imports were also reduced in the difficult winter of 1987 when the GDR experienced production shortfalls.

In reflecting on the GDR-USSR trade relationship, the West German economist, Alfred Schüller, decried the GDR's 'security thinking' with regard to Soviet raw materials and energy. The

---

[21] See M. Haendcke-Hoppe, 'Erfolge und Misserfolge in der Außenwirtschaft', *Die Wirtschaftspolitik der Ära Honecker – ökonomische und soziale Auswirkungen,* Teil 1, 14. Symposion der Forschungsstelle am 17. und 18. November, 1988, *FS Analysen,* Forschungsstelle fuer Gesamtdeutsche und Soziale Fragen, no. 1 (1989) p. 66, Table 6.

[22] The East German Export of ships to the USSR is an important part of this trade. From 1986–1990 deliveries were scheduled to reach 12.5 Billion Valuta-Marks. The GDR was to have produced 180 ships for the USSR by 1990, including 14 completely new types. It is noteworthy, however, that the exports of microelectronic and computer-related products would amount to 14 billion Valuta Marks for that period. See ibid., p. 186.

[23] Haendcke-Hoppe, *op. cit.*, p. 68.

structure of GDR industry reflected the import demands of the Soviets, implying East German forbearance from pursuing its own comparative advantages in world trade. We can readily agree with Schüller that the USSR represented a large seller's market for the GDR, and that this trade relationship led to a structurally undemanding menu of exports and trade provincialism for the highly developed human capital of the GDR economy.[24] But this truth holds whether the Soviets had any direct influence on the GDR's export choices or whether the GDR, given its production limitations, simply chose the Soviet market by default.

The GDR has also been a willing research partner of the Soviets. Between 1980 and 1985, 600 research undertakings were pursued jointly; narrow economic and scientific-technical cooperation with the USSR was alleged to have determined the development of the GDR for a good decade and a half.[25]

As a number of CMEA countries based national agreements more and more on the outcomes of negotiated contracts arising from direct inter-firm relations, the East Germans recognized the necessity of their combines competing against capitalist firms in such contract negotiations. The expanding trade of the Soviets and other CMEA countries with the capitalist countries implied a growing level of competition for Soviet markets.[26] Changes in the Soviet economic mechanism, as well as the changes of some other CMEA countries, forced GDR combines to seek direct contacts to production-level agents in CMEA and capitalist countries. Competitive pressures required that the buyers' demands be considered even before production began, or, as it was surmised with dread, 'profitable trade will no longer be possible'.[27] Other countries, including especially

24 Schueller, *op. cit.*, p. 21.
25 See Engert, *op. cit.*, p. 173.
26 See Käthe Frei, 'Zu den neuen Aspekten der wissenschaftlich-technischen und ökonomischen Zusammenarbeit der RGW-Laender', in Helmut Koziolek, ed., *Sozialistische ökonomische Integration und wissenschaftlich-technischer Fortschritt* (Berlin [East]: Akademie-Verlag, 1988) pp. 41–2.
27 See Sigmund Peter, 'Zu einigen Fragen des Einflußes der Interessen auf die konkreten Formen der Zusammenarbeit', Helmut Koziolek (ed.), *Sozialistischeökonomische Integration und wissenschaftlich-technischer Fortschritt* (Berlin [East]: Akademie-Verlag, 1988) p. 80.

the Federal Republic of Germany, were competitively trying to penetrate the potentially vast Soviet market, and this was seen as relevant to the GDR's own export interests.[28]

Cooperation with the CMEA

The GDR recognized the necessity of considering foreign trade and integration from the perspective of its CMEA membership. The socialist CMEA countries had generally suffered from the same systemic difficulties the East Germans had experienced. The result had been a declining share of world trade for the whole region: in 1980 the CMEA countries conducted 54 per cent of their trade among themselves. In 1986 that amount had increased to 65 per cent.[29] Up to the cataclysm the East Germans were attempting to use what influence they could to address general CMEA economic and trade problems, but they did so with an eye to protecting specific GDR interests in the process of change.

The East German position was that CMEA change should be conservative and cautious. The organization should investigate why the European socialist countries had been almost completely squeezed out of several decisive Western markets characterized by a high degree of scientific-technical progress. That applied to such branches as micro-electronics, computer techniques, mechanical instruments and electrical machine construction. The declining performance apparently stemmed from an insufficient international division of labour within CMEA, beginning with research and continuing through production. This meant that the socialist bloc had not succeeded in achieving the most sophisticated levels of production and had therefore been unable to compete with the capitalist industrial countries or the trade-oriented, newly-industrialized countries. The East Germans having had experience with the broad development and application of key technologies, were convinced

---

28 Ibid., p. 81.
29 Engert, *op. cit.*, p. 172.

that increasing intra-branch specialization between CMEA countries was an absolute necessity.[30] These problems were addressed at CMEA meetings in Moscow (November 1986) and in Berlin (May 1987), and the 'Complex Programme of Scientific-technical Progress of the Member Countries of the CMEA to the Year 2000' was adopted. Its goal was, at a minimum, to double the productivity of social labour by that time. At the 41st (Special) Congress of the CMEA in October 1987, measures were adopted to intensify socialist economic integration for the period 1986–90 and beyond.[31]

At a major conference of the GDR Academy of Sciences in June, 1988, on CMEA integration, the co-ordination of economic plans was cited as the appropriate means for co-ordinating the economic policies of member countries. The intensification of production could be achieved only through an acceleration of scientific-technical progress, an enhancement of social productivity, and reduction of the specific costs of energy and raw materials per unit of national product.[32]

At the 44th session of CMEA, the GDR argued that stability and reliability of mutual economic relationships were of the utmost importance in pursuing increased CMEA integration.[33] In the major

[30] See Willi Kunz, 'Theoretische Fragen der Nutzung der sozialistischen ökonomischen Integration zur Meisterung des wissenschaftlich-technischen Fortschritts', in Koziolek (ed.), *Sozialistische ökonomische Integration und wissenschaftlich-technischer Fortschritt* (Berlin [East]: Akademie-Verlag, 1988) pp. 22, 23.
[31] See Willi Kunz (ed.), *Umfassende Intensivierung – sozialistische ökonomische Integration – Kombinat* (Berlin [East]: Dietz Verlag, 1988) p. 7.
[32] Koziolek, 'Sozialistische Ökonomische Integration' *op. cit.*, p. 7. The theses contain effusive statements on the beneficial effects of SEI (Socialist Economic Integration); it is alleged to play a decisive role in the stable economic and social development of the GDR. It suggests the common responsibility of CMEA members to achieve the development of socialism. SEI is portrayed as an important means of uniting the scientific and economic potential of the socialist states. Aside from such generalities, no quantitative statements or comparative data are offered to demonstrate the substantial benefits claimed.
[33] Willi Kunz, 'Uslovie Stabil'nogo Razvitiya', *Ekonomicheskoe Sotrudnichestvo Stran-Chlenov SEV*, 15, no. 4 (1989) p. 15.

CMEA publication, Willi Kunz, a top GDR spokesman on trade issues, polemicized that the planning process is not an 'evil', but that in socialist conditions and in the relations between socialist countries, economic planning should be considered the main instrument for further economic development.[34]

In the meantime, there was unanimous agreement, largely a product of the influence of Gorbachev, that there must be a restructuring of CMEA and of the mechanisms of multilateral co-operation. The organization was to remain a co-ordinating agency rather than a supranational one, but had to become more flexible and modern.

CMEA members at the time of Honecker's ousting were discussing two very fundamental questions: first, was a completely new conception of international co-operation needed (one in which individual economic units would be the decisive subject of socialist economic integration (SEI)? Second, was the traditional socialist international division of labour so vehemently criticized because it had led to the development of substantially parallel economic structures?[35] Such questions reflected the re-evaluation of all the fundamental tenets of socialist economics, something which continued after the demise of the Honecker economy.

The GDR had participated in three basic types of international co-operation: (1) plan co-ordination, (2) investment participation, and (3) production specialization. Plan co-ordination had always been limited largely to the bilateral specification of commodity exchanges, since the more progressive possibilities for the investments sector remained beyond reach throughout the Honecker era.[36]

---

34 Ibid., p. 17.
35 See M. Engert, 'Anforderungen der wissenschaftlich-technischen Revolution an die internationale sozialistische Arbeitsteilung– Fragen zur Erfüllung des Komplexprogramms des wissenschaftlich-technischen Fortschritts und der Umgestaltung der internationelen Zusammenarbeit', in Helmut Koziolek, ed., *Sozialistische ökonomische Integration und wissenschaftlich-technischer Fortschritt* (Berlin [East]: Akademie-Verlag, 1988) p. 43.
36 Derix and Hoppe, 'Die Außenwirtschaftssysteme', *op. cit.*, p. 218.

Forner advocated more consistent and reliable plan co-ordination. In the past, the results of that process had been captured in protocols, but such protocols were subject to alteration even while the drafts of agreements were still being drawn up. If co-operation issues were completely resolved, breakdowns in agreements could be reduced to a minimum.[37] With increasing diversity in the economic mechanisms of the CMEA countries, Forner insisted, growing diversity in the co-ordination mechanisms would necessarily develop. He also made reference to the need to draw the co-operation of GDR combines and enterprises into the co-ordination process.[38]

GDR Investment participation consisted of (1) financing of supranational projects, (2) compensation arrangements, and (3) contributions to the International Bank for Economic Co-operation. None of these activities functioned at highly significant levels, nor did any contribute noticeably to economic integration. Without a capital market in CMEA, investment participation consisted largely of the direct construction of physical capital and counter trade.[39]

Production specialization, the third form of international co-operation, had been only narrowly developed and remained insufficient. It had concentrated mostly on final goods, rather than on the more integration-intensive specialization in producers goods.[40] Morgenstern criticized the lack of analysis in the development of industrial structure in CMEA's division of labour. Too seldom did projects reflect proper analysis of the material, financial, and intellectual costs of new and continuing measures of scientific-technical co-operation and specialization. Too seldom was it asked whether the possibility existed or could be realized in the requisite time horizon to meet the

---

[37] Andreas Forner, 'Neue Aspekte der Fünfjahrplankoordinierung und Rolle des wissenschaftlich-technischen Fortschritts', Helmut Koziolek (ed.), *Sozialistische ökonomische Integration und wissenschaftlich-technischer Fortschritt* (Berlin [East]: Akademie-Verlag, 1988) p. 68.
[38] Ibid.
[39] Derix and Hoppe, 'Die Aussenwirtschaftssysteme', *op. cit.*, p. 218.
[40] Ibid.

quantitative and qualitative demands of world-market products and services.[41]

Elements of CMEA Strategy: Direct Inter-firm Relations

The history of formal, direct inter-firm relations (DIFR or *Direktbeziehungen*) between GDR and Soviet production units reaches back to January 1967. They were established at that time by an intergovernmental commission on economic and scientific-technical co-operation between the two countries; the agreement called for direct co-operation between central state organs, ministries, and enterprises of both countries.

One of the first ministries to respond to the challenge was the Ministry for Construction, which sent a delegation in January 1967 to the Soviet Union. DIFR were established between the construction and construction materials industries of both countries. Close co-operation was pledged in working out prognoses for construction and in the development of modern methods of managing industrial and housing construction combines.[42] At a similar conference of

---

[41] Karl Morgenstern, 'Zu Wechselbeziehungen zwischen volkswirtschaftlicher Strukturentwicklung und internationaler Arbeitsteilung', Helmut Koziolek (ed.), *Sozialistische ökonomische Integration und wissenschaftlich-technischer Fortschritt* (Berlin [East]: Akademie-Verlag, 1988) p. 73.

But Vanous found some redeeming value in the GDR's previous specialization efforts, writing:

We can see the following pattern in CMEA cooperation: The GDR produces machine tools, programmable machine tools, and industrial robots. Bulgaria specializes in electronic components, while Hungary concentrates on communications and buses. Communications is a growth market in the East bloc. While Czechoslovakia is supplying machinery, nuclear reactors (based on Soviet technology) and factory tools – it is worth noting that no Western country had bet its future on factory tools. The GDR has specialized in goods that are also salable in the West. This seems to have been forgotten in the rest of the CMEA.

See J. Vanous, 'The GDR within CMEA', in 'Symposium on the German Democratic Republic', Irwin Collier (ed.), *Comparative Economic Studies*, 29, no. 2 (Summer 1987), p. 5.

[42] See H. Kanzig, *et al, Wissenschaftlich-technische Zusammenarbeit DDR/UdSSR: Von den Anfängen bis heute* (Berlin [East]: Staatsverlag der Deutschen Demokratischen Republik, 1986), p. 98.

the intergovernmental commission in May of 1968, a review of the co-operation endeavour determined that twenty ministries and other central state organs of the GDR had already drawn up protocols with forty ministries and organs of the USSR for scientific-technical co-operation.[43] Unfortunately, centrally motivated and directed activities of this type never achieved effective levels of economic integration. Although lists of projects and achievements based on DIFR seem to impress CMEA ideologists, these efforts represent but an insignificant fraction of the activities that the interested private agents of market economies would pursue. Nevertheless, as decentralization processes continued to enhance the incentives and decision prerogatives of individual production units, DIFR seemed capable of becoming more meaningful.

As Becker indicated, DIFR applied not only to the combines' interaction with Soviet and other CMEA partners, but also to internal combine relationships within the GDR, which had only begun to develop. That required an expansion of the legal and economic frameworks for the combines to permit them to play an active, responsible role.[44]

A number of organizational forms for the new direct inter-firm relations had been developed. These included:

– planned contracts of managers and specialists of co-operating units;

– formation of temporary groups of specialists or mutual collectives of researchers, developers and construction agents;

– contacts to buyers or users in partner countries, especially in the delivery of technically demanding commodities; and

– co-operation of combines in international organizations.[45]

An interesting CMEA development in direct inter-firm relations was reported by Dubrowsky. Some member countries arranged for

43 Ibid.
44 See Becker, 'Zu neuen Leistungsanforderungen', *op. cit.*, p. 71.
45 See Koziolek, 'Sozialistische Ökonomische Integration', *op. cit.*, p. 16.

authorized agents to deal in specified instances not only in transferable rubles, but also in their own national currency. This was of significance because it extended the range of convertibility, giving the participants experience with limited convertibility. According to Dubrowsky, 'the decision to introduce limited convertibility of national currencies in this area is . . . generally referred to as an experiment'. Experience will show whether the use of national currencies in the place of transferable rubles will bring measurable advantages. Many economists consider the experimental introduction of national currencies in inter-firm direct relations and in some other transactions as a first step toward broader international use of national currencies of the CMEA countries later on.[46]

Under CMEA treaties and arrangements, certain banks were authorized to provide predetermined and limited amounts of national currency for the import payments of approved domestic producers. But the extensive use of national currencies in international exchange would require an equivalence of values, which cannot generally be achieved under regimes of arbitrary pricing. Fundamental barriers to the achievement of equivalence had not yet been overcome, although experiments pertaining to prices and exchange rates were under way.[47] The history of CMEA can demonstrate no successes in this area; on the other hand, the solution of this problem is a trivial matter under regimes of market pricing.

If firms were permitted to develop direct relations (as in the Soviet Union, Poland, Hungary, and in the experimental combines of the GDR), and the firms could collect their own valuta (foreign currency) funds from export earnings, their governments would no longer be able to conclude detailed export and import plans. Enterprises would enjoy an increase in the numbers and variety of commercial partners and their competencies, while for the planning regimes only general contractual arrangements would be possible. But for all the talk of the greater independence and responsibility accruing to East German production units through DIFR, Honecker's

---

46 See Dubrowsky, *op. cit.*, p. 730.
47 Ibid., p. 732.

GDR remained convinced that CMEA direct relations would have to remain subject to the direction of state planning agents.

Elements of CMEA Strategy: Transnational Concerns

In East Europe's effort to 'master the scientific-technological revolution', the trend toward industrial concentration had already produced the 'joint enterprise'. A more recent form of international economic co-operation between two or more socialist countries was the transnational concern. Its advocates within the CMEA offered various organizational conceptions of such concerns, hoping that with greater availability of resources and decision competence, transnational concerns would prove capable of scientific-technical breakthroughs.[48]

The discussion of transnational concerns was an issue in the last months of the Honecker era when the East German economist, Peter,[49] suggested that the GDR should respond to the interests of Soviet partners and agree to form joint enterprises. Especially useful, he thought, could be the establishment of smaller organizations geared toward services. For the GDR, the possibilities for foreign activities were increasingly constrained by labour shortages. Soviet institutes faced a constraint on software for mainframe and personal computers, and since the Soviets were interested in joint enterprises, why not address the problem with joint enterprise software production? Shortly thereafter, the suggestion did in fact produce an organization of the suggested type.

In Leipzig, in March of 1989, an agreement was signed between the two countries for the foundation of a 'joint scientific production centre for the development of software and data processing systems "Zentron".' The partners were the scientific-production association 'Tsentroprogramsystem' Kalinin and the VEB Kombinat Robotron. The organization would be headquartered in Kalinin, and it would develop and introduce programmes applications primarily for electronic data equipment, super-minicomputers, and PCs for various sectors of the economy, e.g. metallurgy, health services, petrol

---

48 See Engert, 'Anforderungen', *op. cit.*, p. 45.
49 Cf. S. Peter, 'Zu einigen Fragen', *op. cit.*, p. 81.

chemistry, and banking. At first this was intended mainly for contracts from the USSR and the GDR, later on, after 'Zentron' became well established, it would also do projects for third countries. The enterprise would function from the outset on the basis of economic accounting, delivering about 250 systems in 1989. Initial capital was to be 5 million TRs, half from each participant. The leading organ of the enterprise was to be a council consisting of three representatives from each country. Branch enterprises of 'Zentron' were to be established in the USSR and the GDR.[50]

Such organization is laudable, of course, but an economic system in which firms passively wait for governmentally sponsored co-operation proposals is not one which can compete with the organizational creativity and diversity of the market economies.

Currency Convertibility

For the more progressive CMEA forces, the convertibility of national currencies was viewed as the principle method of joining the CMEA economies over the long run, as well as the means by which they could be linked monetarily to the world international economic system.

Convertibility would have the advantage of providing an international equivalence through the use of a single value and price measure. It would eliminate the inconvenience of hard currency shortage and of contrived economic relationships with external trading partners (such as the use of countertrade, barter, or other non-monetary transactions). At the same time, convertibility seemed somewhat hazardous to the Honecker regime, because it would open the economy to external influences which would clearly be difficult to plan or manage. To open one's economy to capitalist countries has significant political ramifications, some of which were mentioned above.

Nor would convertibility solve all of socialism's international economic problems. Dubrowsky argued that overcoming bilateralism in

---

50 See S. Baigarov, 'Gemeinsamer Betrieb "Zentron"', *Pravda*, 21 March 1989, cited in *Presse der Sowiet Union*, no. 5 (May 1989), p. 11.

CMEA trade would hardly be achievable through the convertibility of national currencies alone. In addition to replacing the transferable ruble, current commodity shortages in the CMEA countries and in their mutual trade would have to be overcome, exports would have to be stimulated in all the CMEA countries, and domestic and international price formation processes would have to be reformed. [51]

At the top of Dubrowsky's list of prerequisites for currency convertibility was the transformation of the CMEA countries into developed financial economies functioning on the basis of 'commodity-money' (market) relations. That would imply an equilibration of commodity and financial markets, as well as real currency markets. Convertibility would require, second, the ability of CMEA countries to compete in world markets and to maintain sufficient currency reserves. Third, it would necessitate giving production units independence in foreign economic activity.[52] The Dubrowsky article represented the quasi-official East German economic consensus. Honecker era economists believed, however, that these conditions would be achieved only in a distant and nebulous future.

Naturally, a limited degree of convertibility had already been achieved in CMEA tourism and travel even before democratization began to bust the political trusts of East European communist parties; where it is necessary in each country for guests to use the local currency, limited convertibility is the practice. The CMEA countries have accommodated that by reciprocal exchanges of national currencies for payment in transferable rubles. Between CMEA countries there are also multilaterally agreed, uniform rules for limited convertibility in other transactions.[53] In some CMEA countries production units were allowed to retain a portion of their export earnings in currencies and transferable rubles for their own use, or to exchange foreign earnings for their own national currency. In these practices a form of 'inner-CMEA' convertibility had been achieved.

In Poland, Bulgaria, and the Soviet Union, some hard currency

---

[51] See Dubrowsky, *op. cit.*, p. 721.
[52] Ibid, p. 724.
[53] Ibid, p. 729.

auctions occurred at the time of the *Wende*. The state could act as a seller at such auctions, in which case a proxy exchange rate between the domestic and the foreign currencies was established on the basis of supply and demand conditions.[54] The 'real' exchange rates suggested by these auctions made it graphic, as Prouhdon might well have taught, that when the property rights to national currency are the prerogative of Marxist-Leninist governments, foreign exchange is theft.

CMEA currency convertibility was viewed in the economic literature of Honecker's GDR as conceivable only after achieving a general intensification of production. In the pursuit of intensification and convertibility, the production units were to be the carriers of the process. They were, therefore, the agents of socialist economic integration. Direct relations between the producers of the different CMEA countries were viewed as the main avenue of international co-operation. The East Germans also agreed with other CMEA economists that perfecting the economic mechanism and converting to commodity-money (market) relations in exchange would be necessary throughout the CMEA. The effective functioning of the production unit must in fact overcome the conditions of the shortage economy, which obstruct convertibility. More directly prohibitive were the overvaluation of socialist currencies and the danger of opening vulnerable economies (where subsidized necessaries and distorted prices were the implements of social policy) to external economic forces and agents.

A United Market

Quite clearly, the notion of a 'united market' was the East European response to the progressing integration of the European Community's (EC) internal market. Much of the substance of current discussions in the CMEA region and in the individual countries was the result of concern about contemporary developments in the EC as West Europe moved toward increased integrative measures for 1992. In fact, perestroika and the related East European reform

---

[54] Ibid, p. 733.

measures were in part a reflection of the concern of these countries that the economic world was passing them by.

Honecker's GDR was perfectly willing to talk and write about such esoteric developments as a 'united market', but that was much like discussing the arrival of communism, the creation of the new socialist man, or other principles of faith in which scarcely anyone has any. According to the GDR contribution to such literature, there would have to be a stepwise development of conditions permissive of a united market. As those were met, we were assured, the GDR would make its contribution to that development.[55] As was true with convertibility, a united market could be established only on the basis of certain prerequisites, one set of which was listed by Koziolek:[56]

1. Market demands would have to be covered to a high degree, moving CMEA from a seller's to a buyer's market.
2. An equivalence of purchasing power demand and circulating cash would have to be achieved.
3. There would have to be a convergence of the conceptions of CMEA members about participation in the worldwide division of labour. Finally,
4. The social policies of RGW countries would have to be at least minimally harmonized.

Willi Kunz adds to the list of prerequisites for establishing a United Market; he includes working toward convertibility of the transferable ruble, beginning preparations in the meantime for a partial convertibility of RGW countries' currencies within the community; continuing to develop socialist economic integration in the areas of important raw materials and fuels, and pursuing cooperation in important key technologies; continuing to work on direct inter-firm relations.[57]

Dubrowsky was convinced that the way to the united market

---

[55] Cf. H. Koziolek, and O. Reinhold, 'Plan und Markt im System unserer sozialistischen Planwirtschaft', *Einheit*, 44, no. 1 (1989), p. 25.
[56] *Ibid*, pp. 25–6.
[57] See Kunz, 'Theoretische Fragen', *op. cit.*, pp. 29–30.

would be through closer interaction of the socialist economies in the monetary realm. By moving toward mutual convertibility of the national currencies, the CMEA countries could achieve an intensive joining of economic reproduction processes, which would ultimately lead to a currency union and a united market.[58]

With all of its caution and conservatism, taking the position that convertibility and a united market would not be possible until all the CMEA's basic economic problems were peremptorily resolved, Honecker's GDR seemed to be a substantial anti-progressive force in the CMEA organization. Schüller averred that for these reasons the GDR was the decisive constraint (*entscheidende Hemmschuh*) to aspirations for a joint CMEA market. Hungary went so far as openly to advocate a separate solution (without the GDR) to CMEA problems.[59] Given the GDR's ultimate reunification with the Federal Republic, this was a rather prescient suggestion.

TRADE WITH THE FEDERAL REPUBLIC AND THE WEST

East Germany did not fail to recognize before the *Wende*, or turning point, the extreme importance of expanding trade and economic interaction with the West. It had a special advantage, of course, in having favoured trade relations with the Federal Republic, and, as a part of the German 'nation' (consisting of the two German states), also with the EC. While doing all it could to expand hard-currency-generating trade and contacts with a Western clientele, the GDR remained convinced that the specific institution of joint ventures with western countries would not bring returns equivalent to the costs. It remained determined right up to the cataclysm to avoid them. In the new era, however, joint ventures and other forms of western investment participation were destined to become a part of the economic landscape.

On the export side, the past decade began well enough for the East Germans. In the export boomlet of the early 1980s trade had

---

58 Ibid, p. 713.
59 Schüller, *op. cit.*, p. 14.

seemed healthy, and not only with the FRG. As Vanous[60] observed, it is difficult to see through the statistics, even through mirror statistics of partner countries, who the new partners were. But increasing exports of machinery, chemicals, and consumer goods were certainly not all absorbed by West Germany. Expansion of trade with other European states, e.g., Austria, the Benelux nations, France, the U.K. and Sweden, were more impressive than that with the FRG. As the decade wore on, however, the export pace could not be maintained. In Honecker's last years, the GDR's international economic programme had to overcome difficulties other than just the credit crisis. The reduction in Soviet oil deliveries was exacerbated by the decline of the dollar, which was nearly as hard on the GDR as on some of the oil producing countries. By the end of 1986 the GDR had lost at least $1.2 billion, or about half of its gross export receipts from its business with petroleum.[61]

In that period there was a general decline in exports to the West, an indication of the difficulty the GDR experienced in establishing ongoing market shares there. The reduction of exports was balanced in 1987 with a slashing of imports, so that both were around 10 per cent below the previous year. Cornelsen has already called attention to the economic difficulties stemming from this self-imposed restriction of imports of producers goods and capital, which in turn promoted export incapacity.[62]

After this period of decline in trade, it appeared that activity was being stepped up again. The GDR's intense investment demands could only contribute to an increase. In excess of 30 per cent of deliveries to the GDR in 1988 consisted of capital goods. The total of this trade, which represented about half of its Western trade, reached a significantly higher level in the first months of 1989.[63]

---

60 Cf. Vanous, 'The GDR within CMEA', *op. cit.*, pp. 3, 4.
61 See Hoppe, 'Erfolge und Miserfolge', *op. cit.*, p. 57.
62 See D. Cornelsen, 'Die Lage der DDR-Wirtschaft zur Jahreswende 1987/88', *DIW Wochenbericht*, 55 (4 February 1988), p. 65.
63 See Stinglwagner, W., 'DDR-Handel gewinnt an Schwung. Zuversicht nach Messen in Leipzig und Hannover', *Deutschland Archiv*, 22, no. 5 (May 1989), p. 500.

Prospects for Trade with the Federal Republic of Germany.

Trade with the Federal Republic of Germany (FRG) was the other pillar (together with Soviet trade) of the GDR's economic viability. During the credit embargo of the early 1980s, the GDR drastically reduced its imports and pursued an export drive. Imports from the FRG, however, were *not* reduced during this period, which in one West German economist's view may have kept the GDR from 'domestic economic collapse'.[64] In addition, the GDR received two loans from West Germany of 1 billion DM each in the middle of 1983 and 1984, plus

- DM receipts from official intergovernmental payments,
- transit receipts from West Germans, and
- receipts from the required daily minimum currency change for tourists.

Together these receipts summed to 2 billion DM yearly. Together with a plan for prompt payments from export surplus earnings, this revenue permitted payments to be made which assured the reopening of the international credit market for the GDR.

Right up to the cataclysm, the GDR hoped to exploit its special relationship with West Germany and increase significantly the volume of inter-German trade. Both sides were in agreement that trade levels were far below their full potential.[65] The East Germans emphasized that the Federal Republic also stood to benefit from inter-German trade, an assertion which was manifestly true. West German business found that the proximity, the common language, and the established trading relationships made East Germany the preferred socialist trading partner.

The GDR was vocal about its dissatisfaction with barriers to inter-German trade and East-West trade in general. Faithfully mentioned

---

[64] Cf. Hoppe, 'Erfolge und Miserfolge', *op. cit.*, p. 56.
[65] See Jürgen Nitz, 'Wirtschaftsbeziehungen DDR-BRD: Bestimmungs-faktoren, Tendenzen, Probleme und Perspektiven', Beilage zur Wochenzeitung *Das Parlament*, B10 (Bonn: Bundeszentrale für politische Bildung, 3 March 1989), p. 3.

were the abhorred COCOM lists, which from the East German perspective unduly constrained the desired expansion of technological trade. COCOM lists specified the high-tech and other commodities with possible defence applications if exported to East Europe, and forbade trade in such goods. These lists were established by the Western powers and strongly supported by the United States. The turning point was not very far past when President Bush expressed a willingness to reconsider the content of embargoed goods lists and begin a gradual process of relaxation. That would imply greater East-West trade possibilities. Especially painful for the East Germans was the embargo on industrial robots, computers, scientific implements, machines and raw materials required for the production of micro processors, and so on.[66]

But the FRG also had its country-specific trade barriers, the East Germans accused, including quantity and value quotas for a number of commodities of importance for the GDR. These quotas affected the structure and dynamics of inter-German trade. Beyond the *Wende*, the processes of EC integration promised to have a tremendous impact on the economic relationships of the GDR with members of the EC, including the Federal Republic. The GDR believed before and directly after the *Wende*, that this represented a considerable challenge, but also a great opportunity that must be seized.[67]

The GDR believed that eliminating the trade barriers would have been in the interests of both partners, for total trade would surely have increased. FRG exporters would have had opportunities to expand their sales, since the GDR would, under trade liberalization, have been in a position to increase its imports. At the same time, better sales conditions would have been provided for GDR combines.

For the new regime, it was apparent from the outset that rather generous trade and aid flows from West to East Germany would be of critical importance. In the early days of the new era, interim GDR leaders were chiefly concerned that such aid might imply an

---

66 Ibid.
67 Ibid., p. 10.

absorption of the GDR into the Federal Republic. Within an historically very short time, they were fully prepared to accept unification in order to get the capital and assistance that increasingly appeared to be the only way out of the economic decline resulting primarily from the continued flight of GDR labour to the West.

In the last few years of the Honecker era, there was a notable increase in the development of production under license (*Gestattungsproduktion*), the manufacture of brand name commodities of West German firms by East German enterprises.[68] Even before the new era, the two German states perceived a shared interest in the potential benefits of direct co-operation between their firms. Both hoped this would contribute to the long-term stabilization of economic relationships. The co-operation of the Volkswagen concern with GDR combines is well known. But firms of intermediate and smaller size from the Federal Republic began to take up co-operation with GDR enterprises in the last two or so years of the Honecker era.[69]

Prospects for Trade with the West

The GDR was unable to become enthusiastic about Gorbachev's plan to hasten technical progress in the domestic economy through high-tech imports from the West. The GDR's *ancien regime* rejected this idea both because of earlier disappointments in actual experience and because of conceptual considerations. The attempt a decade ago to accomplish this objective resulted only in heavy external debts, and the anticipated modernization effects were not realized. To make another attempt would probably only result in a diversion of resources into consumer goods industries.[70]

The GDR view was that since the West had no desire to enhance the technological strength of socialism, the development of the most

---

[68] Examples are Salamander shoes, Triumph clothing, Trinkfix breakfast drink, Varta batteries, Margaret-Astor cosmetics, Nivea skin cream, as well as products by Adidas and Schiesser. Cf. Nitz, *op. cit.*, p. 10.

[69] Stinglwagner, *op. cit.*, p. 502.

[70] CF. Schüller, *op. cit.*, p. 15.

modern technologies would have to be achieved under socialism's own powers.[71] That attitude motivated the East Germans to build from scratch (without assistance they would have appreciated from CMEA partners) their own computer industry. In doing so, they avoided dependence upon capitalist countries (except for mass pirating of software), and avoided the expenditure of scarce hard currency, acquiring the desired capacity to computerize their machine tool industry. But as one East German economist, a faithful but realistic socialist thinker, confided, this was a technical rather than a commercial achievement.

The effort to enhance export performance continued right up to the end, as could be observed at international trade fairs, but substantive problems persisted as long as Marxist-Leninist socialism did. Even the most competitive products of GDR industry suffered from underdeveloped marketing and delivery inconsistency, which reflected continuing capacity bottlenecks. Nor were the excessive bureaucratic obstacles hindering inter-firm cooperation overcome.[72]

CONCLUSIONS: LONGING FOR PAST CMEA GLORY

Consider now the implications of the GDR's international economic relationships under Honecker for the GDR economy after the counter-revolution of 1989. Before Gorbachev's reforms disturbed the more calm and secure era of (economically collapsing) socialism in East Europe, the GDR had basically learned how to cope successfully with the challenge of orthodox and centralized economic planning of the type Brezhnev favoured. Having through diligence and creativity become the leading performer in the static socialist community, East Germany had to watch aghast as powerful and influential partners began to pursue policies which might ultimately be responsible for dismantling that community. Chief villain in this

---

71 Engert insists that for these reasons technology cannot be imported, but that even if it were possible to do so, that would not be a long-term solution. The capacity to innovate must be pursued with all of socialism's resources. See Engert, 'Anforderungen', *op. cit.*, p. 44.
72 Stinglwagner, *op. cit.*, pp. 500, 501, and 503.

drama was, of course, the Soviet Union, which hitherto had had no more faithful ally than the GDR.

Becoming increasingly isolated, the Honecker establishment looked back upon the past with nostalgia and forward with misgivings. A competent economic establishment sought to come to grips with the need for continuing and signifcant change (they never felt they had completed the required improvements for their economic mechanism), but they were hampered by political constraints which became increasingly hazardous. The international environment was forcing more change on the GDR than it felt comfortable in accepting. Its refusal to come to grips with change in CMEA and in world markets made it increasingly an economic anachronism.

In the long term, they knew they must face the possibility that revolutionary change would become inevitable. It was probably inevitable whether or not Gorbachev's perestroika proved successful. A socialism built on the old economic foundations seems peremptorily to have proved itself untenable. But in the short term, the GDR's economic capacity to resist reform seemed better than outsiders could surmise. Politically, the SED gave signals to its people that it was not prepared to accept demands for liberalization. In the official East German view, China was the model for retaining law and order and dealing with counter-revolutionary forces. How could Honecker know that Krenz would rescind the order to open fire on dissent?[73]

Economically, external pressure for reform could be rather conveniently withstood so long as the Soviet pace of development retained its current sluggishness. The Soviets continued to waffle in the implementation of price reform; nor, in spite of the rhetoric, had the Soviets really achieved many of their other more conservative reform objectives. If one looked all the way back to 1980, the GDR, while talking far less, had *achieved* more actual change than the Soviets.

---

[73] At the time of writing, it is not clear how history will treat the question which appears to have led to Honecker's removal. It does appear that the order was given to fire on demonstrators. Thankfully, the Chinese solution was not applied.

The CMEA was in limbo, waiting to see what happened in the USSR. And so long as large numbers of Soviet troops remained in East Europe (the withdrawal even at the end of the Honecker era had been symbolic), the GDR could continue to live in the world of the past.

From the West, the pressure of relentless change was also too great to overlook and the East Germans needed to worry about the increasing competitiveness of western markets and the changing environment that EC integration represented. But while the long-term effects of such change remained uncertain, the key relationships with the Federal Republic remained intact. Payments from the West German federal budget continued to flow, credits were granted, and new trade opportunities seemed possible. Although this special relationship had its problem areas, it nevertheless represented a powerful element of stability in the short run. So the situation of the GDR seemed perfectly tenable until shortly before the fortieth anniversary celebration.

The cataclysm began insidiously with the brazen removal of Hungarian barbed wire, destroying the integrity of the border with imperialism. It was promoted with the Soviet refusal to intervene to prevent the haemorrhage of refugees to the West. It ripened with the full recognition by the East German people of the power of their position. Thus, political management slipped out of the hands of the party.

What did the economic future have in store? A euphoric populace having been mistrained and misinformed regarding economic reality might have had to wander in the desert for a period of time before it would be prepared to enter the promised economic land. It was not easy to break the inertia of Honecker's economic establishment. Modrow's government was new, but the faces of the participants were all well known from the Honecker years. People who seemed never to have had a reform thought were now labeled as 'reformers'.

A reformist opposition favouring market relationships exists in Hungary and Poland, but had to be developed in East Germany, where no economist was prepared before October of 1989 to admit any positive feelings about markets, let alone a proclivity to bourgeois economics. On the basis of the early Modrow pronouncements (to be discussed in Chapter 4) one could expect that dramatic economic change would have been slow in coming. GDR economists and planners were anxious to pursue closer integration with the CMEA region, and to expand its economic interaction with the West. But under the new conditions prevailing in East Europe, progress required a period of education for all segments of East German society. They read developing events correctly, however, surmising that there would be little substantive change if the new version of the party were left unpressured to select its own pace. The East Germans did, therefore, apply relentless pressure for change. The continuing demonstrations and the continuing mass exodus to West Germany hastened the discussion and planning for reform and got a scheduled May election moved up to March of 1990.

4 The GDR Economy After the Turning Point: on Shortages and Reform Conceptions

As is usually the case under socialism, the GDR economy under Honecker was a shortage economy. After the opening of the borders, supply gaps increased in severity; but the shortages were not merely the result of emigration. They also existed, firstly, because of the functioning of a central planning apparatus, and, secondly, because of the the party's decade-long practice of channeling resources away from productive investments into consumer goods production. As a consequence of these problems, the post-Honecker economy suffered from rather considerable supply gaps. These were in the areas of (1) consumer goods and services, (2) raw materials, (3) intermediate goods, (4) capital goods, (5) export goods, (6) foreign currency, (7) labour, (8) management, and (9) market-oriented economists. The purpose of this chapter is to discuss the nature of the shortages, to illuminate their implications, and to attempt an overall assessment of GDR economic prospects beyond the *Wende*.

When we speak of shortage, we refer to something other than the general notion of scarcity, the situation which normally exists for any socially desired commodity or service in any (capitalist or socialist) economy. Scarcity is what causes a commodity to bear a positive price in an exchange situation. In contrast, shortage exists when at the prevailing price the quantity supplied by a given market is insufficient to satisfy the quantity demanded.

As the new conditions in East Germany generated new societal demands, and 'prices' began to change; as enterprise managers were given greater independence, managers with entrepreneurial skills were found to be in short supply. Likewise, movement away from centrally oriented planning demonstrated that the GDR was lacking in economists with expertise in the functioning of markets. These new shortages took their place alongside the old ones.

Since both the new and more traditional shortages were of extreme importance, in the first section we shall consider more specifically the nature and implications of both types. In the second section our attention will turn to the efforts of the interim government to address the shortages and their causes, reviewing the conceptual discussion of possible change and the actual reform programme proposed by Prime Minister Modrow. We shall also discuss the insufficiencies of the programme, i.e., the gaps between this rather traditional East European reform approach and the long-term objectives actually motivating the party.

SHORTAGE CONDITIONS IN THE GDR ECONOMY

Labour

Shortages were prevalent even before heavy emigration began in late 1989. In part, this was because firms use labour inefficiently in central planning regimes. They tend to requisition all they can get from the centre, since managers perceive labour's marginal cost to the enterprise to be zero. Additional workers can always be used because of the phenomenon of 'storming' (heavy utilization of all available labour in the final part of any planning period, usually each month). Storming's desperate, last-minute effort is to meet physical planning targets and secure bonuses before a deadline. Managers often hoard labour, employing more than would be required for other than 'peak-load' periods of effort.

In the GDR case, increasing numbers of workers were also required for repair work on industry's dilapidated machinery and equipment. This is another reflection of the inadequate volume of investments in Honecker's last years. By 1989, fully 17 per cent of all employees in manufacturing industry and energy production (280,000 workers) were engaged in repair work.

The flight of labour late in 1989 brought down the Wall and left many work sites undermanned. The GDR entered the reform era with roughly a quarter of a million fewer people (up to November the government was willing to admit only to 90,000 emigrants).[1] In the whole of 1989 approximately 340,000 left the GDR permanently; of these, about 225,000 were employed. With reference to total employment of about 9.5 million (including some not reflected in official statistics), that represented a loss of approximately 2.4 per cent of the GDR's labour force. Nor was the outflow of people stopped with the dismantling of the wall. Before and after 9 November, emigrants included a disproportionate share of younger workers and workers from rather severely stricken branches (e.g., doctors, medical care personnel, trade and other service providers, as well as workers from industry and construction in general). Because of the size and composition of the losses, some production bottlenecks were inevitable.

It was doubtful in the extreme that these gaps could be overcome through the recruitment of foreign workers, who usually require training before becoming effective. The GDR had already employed c. 152,000 guest workers, of which 88,000 were from Vietnam, Mozambique, Cuba, Poland, Angola, and China;[2] it was unlikely that it would be possible to increase that number much. So at the *Wende* the labour haemorrhage represented an element of uncertainty for the stability of domestic economic processes in the near term.

Raw Materials and Energy

Continual shortage conditions held for nearly all types of raw materials in East Germany. Lignite was an exception, but its open-pit mining was subject to weather vagaries and increasing cost conditions. As the decisive primary energy source it was inefficiently utilized in the generation of electric power, which was also generally squandered. Unfortunately, the insatiable consumption of lignite caused massive environmental problems. Another critical supply condition existed in the case of water. The low level of supply reflected the severe pollution of water streams from industrial effluents.

---

1   Cf. *Tribüne*, 7 November 1989, p. 2.
2   Ibid., p. 3.

Intermediate Goods

Raw materials, equipment, parts, and intermediate products had already been in short supply for years before the turning point. The complicated and bureaucratic central supply system, based on material balancing, was simply not capable of delivering unfinished products in sufficient volume, with satisfactory quality, or with acceptable punctuality. Even worse, a number of outputs were of materials-intensive production. That resulted not only in higher costs and insufficient international competitiveness, but also in inflated values which gave an upward bias to the indices of production and economic growth.

Capital Goods

In the face of strongly constrained investment capacities the GDR was not able to provide sufficient resources for the investments that would be required to reach the various goals of the economy. At the same time, however, the aggregate of gross fixed assets was extremely high (in 1988 it was M1685 billion in 1986 prices, and in 1989 it was M1750 billion). That amounted to M177,000 per worker in the productive branches as of 1988 (increasing to about M186,000 in 1989), which was not too far below the Federal Republic. The productivity of labour and capital were, however, only about half as high as in West Germany.[3] The difference was attributable in part to the (only directly productive) stock of buildings and the differing sectoral structures of the two economies. Moreover, the GDR capital stock had become remarkably aged. Equipment in the manufacturing industry (plus the mining and energy industries) had the following age structure in 1989: 27 per cent was up to five years old, 52 per cent was up to twenty years old, and 21 per cent was more than twenty years old.[4] A high-cost attempt was made to keep the capital stock in sufficient repair to meet plan

---

[3] Cf. *Materialien zum Bericht zur Lage der Nation im geteilten Deutschland 1987*. Bundestagsdrucksache 11/11, 18 February 1987, pp. 294, 295, and 479.

[4] See *Die Wirtschaft*, Heft 3 (1990) p. 19.

targets, but much of it should have been scrapped long before the *Wende*.[5] In 1980 the industrial branches continued producing with M58 billion worth of machinery and equipment that had been fully amortized. By 1989 the sum of such equipment had reached M133 billion. That corresponded to a share of about 20 per cent of the total capital stock (it had been 14 per cent in 1980). One should keep in mind that the GDR permitted only modest and constant amortization rates, setting the normative duration of capital utilization extraordinarily high.

For that share of the stock of more recent vintage, excessively high costs were also incurred because of the tardiness of its completion, the inefficient planning and co-ordination of its development and use, and the frequent high degree of its technological obsolescence.

Consumer Goods and Services

Partial gaps in consumer goods and services supplies were commonplace, especially because the composition of such goods was specified by the economic leadership. Preferences were too often biased toward a menu that was familiar, almost traditional, and therefore oriented to the past. The desires of the consumers and export clientele were largely neglected.

This condition had been widely recognized, even in socialist societies, as at least partially responsible for the inadequate motivation of workers. This was especially pitiable in a country whose principle claim to economic fame over the last decade had been the 'unity of social and economic policy',[6] an implied, self-imposed commitment to reward worker effort at the retail outlet. Consumers in fact were confined to lower levels of well-being when those goods that were available in sales outlets provided less satisfaction than those which

---

5 Published data verify this statement. See 'Zur Lage der Volkswirtschaft der DDR', *Neues Deutschland*, 11 January 1990, p. 3.

6 See P. J. Bryson, '*Sozialpolitik*: East German Social Welfare Policies', *Comparative Economic Studies*, vol. 28, no. 2 (1986) pp. 1–20, and 'GDR Economic Planning and Social Policy in the 1980s', *Comparative Economic Studies*, vol. 29, no. 2 (1987), pp. 19–38.

were desired but were not available.[7] At the same time, the production of obsolete and low-quality goods incapable of attracting consumers diverted resources from other, more rewarding uses. Large stocks of such 'unloadable' commodities, which up to the *Wende* still counted as productive activity for enterprises, were a socialist producers' luxury that the GDR could no longer afford.

Increasingly, the GDR has experienced disproportionalities between 'purchasing funds' and 'commodity funds' (purchasing power and purchasable goods and services), with the resultant excess demands providing unwelcome inflationary pressure.[8] From 1986 to 1989 the net monetary receipts of the populace were M636 billion. Purchases of goods and services accounted for an expenditure of M561 billion, M32 billion were for insurance and taxes, and savings claimed M42 billion. With this sum the stock of savings and private money holdings for 1989 reached M177 billion, which was an increase of 28 per cent over 1985. In an economy that aspired to a relaxation of central controls on prices, this large inflationary potential was of great concern.

Hard Currency

The GDR's chronic shortage of convertible currencies was the product of: (1) limited export capacity, (2) international credit obligations to western countries, and (3) growing demands (even in CMEA trade) for hard currency payments for certain goods. The pressure to generate foreign currency was destined to grow dramatically once the right to travel in the West had been vouchsafed East Germans. The system had not, of course, gained any capacity to generate hard currency independently just because Honecker's regime disappeared. It must be observed that the GDR had a large net indebtedness of about $18.5 billion. This figure is larger than had earlier been estimated by Western experts, but it was not

---

7 Cf. I. Collier, 'The Measurement and Interpretation of Real Consumption and Purchasing Power Parity for a Quantity Constrained Economy: The Case of East and West Germany', *Economica*, vol. 56 (February 1989) pp. 109–20.
8 'Zur Lage der Volkswirtschaft', *op. cit.*

so high as to make the GDR an unreliable partner in international trade.

Export Goods

The foreign trade situation was characterized by an insufficiency of export goods. On the one hand, that was the result of the lag in the technological performance of GDR products. On the other hand, it was the result of the GDR's ties to CMEA trade partners rather than to world markets. The CMEA countries were long ago transformed by socialist shortages and producer indifference into sellers markets permissive of low quality and dated technology. For an industrial country like the GDR, the level of participation in the international division of labour was most inadequate. It was vital that the old autarkic bias of central planning be eliminated as soon as possible so that the inefficiencies, commodity shortages, and high cost of self-supply could be overcome.[9] Only by changing autarkic proclivities and by dropping fully unprofitable exports could the objective of a favourable foreign currency exchange relationship be achieved.

The shortage of hard currencies had a rather devastating impact on imports, prohibiting the acquisition of badly needed technology-laden equipment from abroad. Such items were too often refused by the state or were subject to COCOM list exclusion. The discontinuities of production often made immediate imports of intermediate goods essential; consumer goods bottlenecks suggested immediate resort to imports. Moreover, a high share of the imports from CMEA countries were goods of little processing or of very modest quality standards, being the result of long-term trade arrangements. Frequently, such intermediate goods could not be used for the upgraded production processes that exportable goods required. Still, the satisfaction of raw materials and energy demands through imports from the CMEA region was an important element of the stability of the GDR's foreign economic sector.

---

9 Cf. *Der Morgen*, 2 November 1989.

Although from 1981 to 1985 an export surplus of 26 billion Valuta Marks (VM)[10] was achieved, the balance as of 1990 was negative. That was due especially to the decline of exports to the non-socialist economies as the export efficiency of the GDR drastically declined.

Management

There had been an ongoing, concerted attempt in the GDR to develop a pool of managerial talent. While the Soviets were continually talking *Khozraschet* (or 'economic accounting', which is an attempt to make enterprises function profitably, paying their own costs rather than subsisting on subsidies), the East Germans were busy implementing it. Through periodical executive training seminars, intensive efforts were made to train managers of combines and enterprises. Institutes for Socialist Economic Management (*Sozialistische Wirtschaftsführung*) at the university level provided training for enterprise managers, while the party's Central Committee had a Central Institute for Economic Management which provided training for combine managers. Gunter Mittag, the politburo's economics specialist through most of the Honecker era, met personally with all of the Republic's combine directors when they assembled once each year.

Both those giving and receiving such training were motivated and competent individuals. Before the turning point, combine managers bore very heavy responsibility without exceptional rewards. They received a company car and a chauffeur, and could lay claim to a few extra privileges (such as avoiding the queue for automobiles and housing), and they generally earned only four or five times more than the least skilled labourers on the plant floor. But that

---

10 Valuta Marks are foreign exchange earnings expressed in East German marks. VM represent an exchange rate whose value is expressed in terms of the GDR Mark. It is calculated by the State Bank of the GDR strictly for the purposes of foreign trade. In 1989 it was 1DM = M4.4, in 1986 1DM = M3.6, and in 1985 1DM = M2.9. This demonstrates graphically how rapidly domestic costs for 1 DM worth of imports increased in trade with the Western countries.

was basically the extent of it; and they often had responsibility for numerous thousands of workers in plants spread over a large portion of the country.

Considerable emphasis was laid on having the managers of the larger enterprises operate with as much independence as possible. Interviews with a number of combine DGs and enterprise managers was an eye-opening experience for anyone expecting these individuals to follow the classical Soviet model, where managers took precious little initiative, had training in engineering rather than business management, and wanted merely to put together inputs to get a target-satisfying output, regardless of the quality level involved.[11] Many of the GDR managers were comfortable with a rather hard budget constraint, and a number indicated that although improvements must still be achieved, even the plant managers of many multiple-plant enterprises (often some distance from headquarters) also enjoyed a rather surprising degree of independence.

This is not to say that GDR managers had nothing more to learn as they entered the post-Honecker era. They needed to continue their adjustment to greater responsibility and greater risk as interaction with the market economies of West and East Europe increased. Marketing techniques were bound to become significant, most enterprises still had to be weaned from state subsidies, and the full brunt of production costs (inclusive of growing external costs) had to be borne. There was a deficit in experience in dealing with this new, less secure managerial environment. It seemed likely, however, that the East Germans would

---

[11] Bryson had the opportunity to engage in such interviews in the spring of 1985 and again in the spring of 1989. He will not soon forget the necessity of casting off the inclination to believe these were low-level functionaries incapable of and unwilling to make significant decisions responsibly, even in the face of substantive risk. He remembers one producer of shoes that are exported and sold under the Salamander label in West Germany; after having learned about responsible and creative enterprise management and the fundamentals of shoe production, Bryson greatly enjoyed a little comradely enlightenment on such matters as the literature of Goethe and an evaluation of current international relations.

be able to adapt very quickly and effectively to the new conditions in which they had to operate.

Market-oriented Economists

Traditionally, the Hungarians and Poles have had a strong minority of neo-classical, 'bourgeois' economists. Some of the famous names in the discipline came from these countries, and these scholars and their successors could provide the intellectual support for systemic change. The East Germans were not so endowed, however, having eliminated 'troublemakers' early on. Economists in Honecker's GDR were bright, hard-working and creative types. But if there were closet 'bourgeois' who carried any secret toleration for markets, they were able to keep it completely secret.

It was to be expected beyond the *Wende* that the academic economists would learn very quickly how to respond to the exigencies of a more market-oriented environment. Given GDR tradition and culture, however, in the attempt to reform central planning, these individuals would rather be inclined to emphasize the 'central' rather than the 'reform'.

Minister President Modrow's Vice Prime Minister and Economics Minister, Christa Luft, was representative of the orientation of the academic establishment. Formerly Rector of the University of Economic Science, 'Bruno Leuschner', in East Berlin and a member of the Scientific Council of the Academy of Sciences, Prof. Luft, writing before the cataclysm, was accepting of greater independence and self-management for production units. After all, that development had become a given for economists in the CMEA region. She was certainly not enamoured with markets, however. A specialist in international economics, she had become convinced through practical experience that the 'best possible use of the proportionality – and efficiency-generating aspects of foreign economic relationships' could not be achieved through increased international responsibility for production units functioning in an 'isolated' way from each other. Such firms certainly could not 'be left to spontaneous market forces'.[12] Luft saw no conflict between self-management and central state direction and planning of external affairs. In her view the centre must perform the function of co-ordination, thereby ensuring the inner proportionality of the economy, and it must safeguard the greater interests of society as a whole. The centre must (1) accept responsibility for a higher level of long-term strategic work, (2) guide the domestic producers to beneficial trade relationships by creating appropriate long-term normatives and other framework conditions, and (3) give consideration to the requirements of the foreign sector in the design of planning coefficients.[13]

Before Honecker's cataclysm, GDR economists, like Luft, were continually pursuing means of rationalizing the system of central planning. They were not unwilling to try to speak the language of reformers in other CMEA countries who had thrust such concepts as currency convertibility, enterprise independence, and a unified market into the centre of discussion for CMEA's socialist economists. But they seemed uncomfortable with the changing world; they shied away from making peace with market allocation and sought to ensure the continuity of stable and secure planned relationships among socialist economies. Under relentless pressure, however, both from the rapidly deteriorating economy and from the East German public (which continued well after the *Wende* to conduct its peaceful weekly demonstrations and refused fully to trust even the 'reform' Communist and interim Premier, Hans Modrow), the interim Vice Premier adopted a reform stance that would have been unimaginable even a short time earlier. It was to be expected that other economists and planners of former SED orientation would follow suit. That they did so became apparent through a public discussion of the role of enterprises and marketization shortly after Honecker's retirement.

---

12 Christa Luft, 'Entwicklungstendenzen', *op. cit.*
13 Ibid., p. 54.

THE CONCEPTUAL BASES OF REFORM:
THE ENTERPRISE AS THE KEY

In a situation characterized by rather severe and ongoing supply shortages, it was apparent that the industrial combines were in a powerful market position before and after the *Wende*. GDR suppliers were able to dominate markets even if they were not formally monopolies, though in fact they too often were in a clear monopoly position in their given production area. It was, therefore, relatively easy for them to impede innovation; moreover, in a reform environment moving away from central price direction, they would not have to worry much about restricting outputs to facilitate higher prices.

The creation of substantially increased competition (via the dismantling of the relevant combines) was vitally necessary. GDR producers too frequently introduced specious novelty into their product lines; the increased prices attached to pseudo-quality improvements regularly exceeded the magnitude of associated improvements. There could be no competitive response and the planning authorities, oriented to rapid growth, showed no concern.

After the *Wende*, some of the leading GDR economists began immediately to express their views as to the necessity and nature of economic reform. Helmut Richter[14] explained quite correctly that the focus of economic reform must be the individual enterprise, regardless of the organizational *milieu* (e.g., as a combine member). In his view, the enterprise had three decisive tasks: first, to produce to meet consumer demands; second, to function profitably; and third, to create working and living conditions that would 'permit the functioning of the achievement principle (*Leistungsprinzip*)'.[15] Socialism could no longer afford to reward workers on a primarily egalitarian basis, but simply had to consider what a worker actually achieved.

---

14 Formerly Director of the Institute of Socialist Management at East Berlin's University of Economic Science, Richter was prevailed upon by Modrow to assume the direction of the former 'Koziolek' Institute, now the Institut für Unternehmensführung.
15 Helmut Richter, 'Wie unsere Wirtschaft leiten? *Neues Deutschland*, 17 November 1989, p. 5.

Uwe Schmidt of the Academy of Sciences insisted that enterprises must 'orient their activities to consumer demands rather than to an economic plan. A functioning market mechanism is therefore essential'.[16] Helmut Voigt was even clearer in suggesting that private firms be created in light industry. He reminded his colleagues that one should not speak of incapable managers and labour collectives, but of 'disfranchised and regimented' enterprise personnel. The potential in GDR enterprises for effective market participation had not begun to be tapped, let alone exhausted.[17]

How far the discussion of the question of creating competition and independent firms had progressed was demonstrated by GDR spokesmen after the *Wende*. Helmut Richter, this time writing in a Western periodical, observed that the deciding reform issue was the enterprise functioning on its own responsibility. To him the term 'firm' meant 'the co-operative, the half-state-owned firm, the mixed firm, and the private, capitalistic firm, the handicraft enterprise, and the large combine, all of which will be permitted again in the GDR'.[18]

Juergen Kuczynski, the veteran of GDR political economists, pulled the discussion together very capably with perceptive observations. When more market orientation is demanded for the GDR economy, he observed, one thinks especially about the huge production units. The combines and their component enterprises must finally lose their monopoly positions. Strict and honest economic accounting for monopolies would achieve some desired effects, but could not achieve enough. What was really required in GDR industry was competition among enterprises; they must bring competing outputs to a developed wholesale market and also make purchases in that market.[19] The creation of competition

---

16 Cf. Uwe Schmidt, 'Die Wirtschaftsreform – brisanter denn je', *Der Morgen*, 17 November 1989, p. 3.
17 See Helmut Voigt, 'Betriebsplanung ohne Direktiven', *Neues Deutschland*, 28 December 1989, p. 5.
18 See Helmut Richter, 'Wir Müßen jetz brutal die Wahrheit sagen', *Die Welt*, 23 November 1989, p. 18.
19 Jürgen Kuczynski, 'Schluß mit dem Monopolsozialismus', *Neues Deutschland*, 28 December 1989, p. 5.

between independent firms would also require the introduction of some type of anti-trust legislation, so that competition could be firmly established for the long term.

An improvement of industrial supply processes would necessitate, in addition to the restructuring of the enterprises, the establishment of an effective wholesale trade system in producers' and intermediate goods. The logical concomitant to this would, of course, be the gradual elimination of material balancing. That would in turn permit a healthy reduction of another associated practice, which was prevalent in the combines before the *Wende*, although seldom meaningful in terms of economic efficiency, *viz.*, that of the in-house construction of much of the equipment required for modernization purposes.

Such were East German thoughts on economic change at the beginning of the reform era; their free expression was long overdue. One could only wonder whether the liberation of economists from the pervasive party influence in East Germany would produce bold enough results. After the turning point, arbitrary prices severely limited the effectiveness of resource utilization; modest worker motivation and insufficient numbers of workers constrained growth; simplified channels of information, instruction, and command had established monopoly positions for gargantuan production organizations; shortages of productive resources and of various consumer goods and services reflected the ineptness of planning. Worst of all, these conditions tended to hasten the flight of the disillusioned; the consequent labour shortages and political disarray threatened to undermine the viability of the whole economy.

WHAT KINDS OF REFORMS WERE NEEDED AND POSSIBLE AFTER THE TURNING POINT?

If whatever economic reform the GDR had undertaken were successful, that would be reflected in a reduction of the shortages discussed above. The reform design would have to be broad and comprehensive to promise success. When reform entered into public discussion in East Germany, it was with the anticipation that the country would have to try to recoup from its labour losses and system deficits and move forward, basically independently. Perhaps, outside assistance from the Federal Republic and/or other Western countries might be available. What was not foreseen at that time, however, was that there would be almost immediate pressure from the populace to seek reunification with West Germany as a solution to the growing economic misery.

After reunification suddenly became inevitable, the notion of reform was rather academic, but not completely so. In the transition from socialism to reunification, reform could be the social catalyst for retaining purpose and order. It could serve as a means to prepare East German human resources to function within the framework of a 'social market economy'. Social welfare policies play an important role in the Federal Republic, but the principle resource allocation mechanism is the market. Scarce East German resources needed to be allocated with the greatest efficiency possible. System designers (in this case, 'reformers') would also hope to use the interim prior to the achievement of a reunified Germany as a crash course in preparing the populace to function in a market environment. The Modrow government sought throughout its brief term to continue its thrust toward reform, not only considering possible reform measures (as we shall see in this chapter), but also passing legislation (as we shall see in the next) which would partially remain in force until reunification was achieved, although generally unnoticed and unimplemented in the period prior to that.

A final reason for discussing these last reforms is that the laws suggested and drafted looked much like tank traps to hinder the wholesale adoption of West German law (which occurred anyway).[20] A frantic attempt was made by the party, if only for that short interim, to avert reunification with the Federal Republic by establishing a reform programme that would convince East Germans that the GDR was still viable as an independent political entity. That whole programme casts a penetrating light on the pervasive inadequacies of the SED's planning system. It also demolishes the insufficiency of the conceptions the SED's successor party, the party of Democratic

---

[20] From the anonymous correspondence of a colleague (gratefully received in October 1989) more than willing to help assure that any misleading exposition be nipped in the bud.

Socialism (PDS), could generate to address a deteriorating economic system and situation. These considerations make a review of the abortive reform effort especially interesting.

In the period of open discussion on reform, GDR authors listed the following as important components of a programme: 'the economic strategy, the determination of goals and criteria of economic and social development, as well as fundamental changes in the economic mechanism. i.e., directing, planning, and economic accounting'.[21] Otto Reinhold, Rector of the Academy of Social Sciences of the Central Committee of the SED, even after Honecker's ouster, was still speaking of a 'market-oriented planned economy' in which the influence of the market would be expanded, but in which the planning processes would not be relinquished; rather, they would be 'restricted to key areas'.[22]

Caspar Schirmeister observed that the new economic mechanism, which must be designed to be conducive to innovative performance, 'must be compatible not only with the changing economies of the socialist countries, especially, of course, of the Soviet Union, but also with the leading capitalist countries.[23] That implied the achievement of a greater capacity for adaptation both to the internal EC market and to (the then prevailing conceptions of) a viable CMEA market.

The goal of economic reform of the GDR was to create a production structure capable of servicing more effectively both domestic consumer demands and the demands of world markets. One hoped with the achievement of this objective to reduce the productivity gap between the GDR and the west. On average that gap *vis-à-vis* the Federal Republic amounted to at least 50 per cent, which was roughly the same as the gap in living standards.

In a formal government declaration of policy intent (*Regierungserklärung*), the Modrow government provided a list of the characteristics a reformed East German economy needed to assume

---

21 Cf. Wofgang Heinrichs and Wolfram Krause, 'Wirtschaftsreform – Element der Erneuerung des Sozialismus', *Neues Deutschland*, 3 November 1989, p. 4.
22 *Frankfurter Allgemeine Zeitung*, 7 November 1989, p. 19.
23 Cf. 'Wirtschaftsreform ja – aber wie?' (Diskussion mit Prof. Dr C. Schirmeister), *Junge Welt*, 7 November 1989, p. 3.

if it were to bring about the essential economic transformation.[24]

1. *Decentralization.*   In keeping with the spirit of the times in East Europe, increased independence was to be granted to enterprises and combines. Modrow spoke of more individual responsibility (*Eigenverantwortung*) and more room for manoeuvre (*Spielraum*) for managers. More emphasis was to be placed on profitability as an incentive for enhanced performance. Decision-making opportunities, e.g., regarding investments, alterations in production processes, and, of course, activities in the international economic realm, were to be expanded.

2. *Diminished planning scope.* This would imply a reduced number of planning coefficients and norms. The rigid 'formula approach' to ministerial direction of enterprises would at least partially be eliminated, and monitoring agencies would be discontinued or left with fewer functions. The intent was to overcome or drastically reduce the excessive intervention which was commonplace in the pre-cataclysm economic order.

3. *Modified central supply system.*   Planning (through the inflexible and unresponsive balancing system) was to be modified.

4. *Improved worker motivation.*   An attempt to achieve higher levels of performance was promised, particularly through clearly differentiated wages and premiums. This was considered of central importance.

5. *Greater flexibility for the economy.*   Not only did this prospect promise that greater efficiency could be achieved, but that the economy could also be opened to the international division of labour.

While these objectives may promise some gains in efficiency, there was nothing really new here; the 'reformer' Modrow was not

---

[24] Cf. Hans Modrow, 'Diese Regierung wird eine Regierung des Volkes und der Arbeit sein', *Neues Deutschland*, 18/19 November 1989, p. 3ff.

likely to be able with this approach to teach anything to the GDR's economic intelligentsia. Nor was this a mature and complete menu of reform concepts; the central question of pricing, for example, was not addressed.

It should be observed that the plan targets for 1989 were not achieved, in large measure because the balancing of intermediate products did not permit closure of the supply gaps. Nor could the plan for 1990 be balanced, since the necessary foreign trade acquisitions were too extensive; also, of course, changes in priorities implied substantial adjustment problems. Regarding the five-year plan 1991 to 1996, Gunther Kohlmey[25] expressed the belief that it would be impossible in 1990 to determine immediately the necessary qualitative and quantitative path of economic development over the next quinquennium.

In Kohlmey's view, if the intent to develop economic democracy were to be taken seriously one would have to take into account the opinions of a number of institutions, groups, and individuals. Views would have to be be solicited and carefully considered. The debate would have to consider all sorts of possibilities, since the GDR would have had to ask seriously what developments in the EC market implied, how more co-operation might be achieved with Western trade partners, and what could be done with the balance of payments and international credits. The answers to these questions, Kohlmey emphasized, could not simply be swallowed whole by a five-year plan that might be prepared in 1990.[26]

MODROW'S SHORT-TERM PROGRAMME FOR THE STABILIZATION OF THE GDR ECONOMY

To achieve a conception of reform and to consider the synchronization of proposed measures, the Ministerial Council formed

---

[25] Cf. Gunther Kohlmey, 'Fünfjahrplan 1991–1995?' *Neues Deutschland*, 18/19 November 1989, p. 10.
[26] Ibid.

eleven task force groups to discuss economic problems. Their ideas became the foundation of the more developed, actual reform programme to be considered later. These groups worked under time pressure and some suggestions were published very early.[27] Numerous additional authors from widely varying institutional backgrounds contributed to a rather open discussion. The nascent party and political groupings were also anxious to participate in the development of conceptions for desirable reforms.

Given the fluid political conditions, the gaping divergence of opinions expressed, and the extreme difficulty of the problems of economic transformation (e.g., the timing and dosage of reform medicines), it remained impossible for some time after the turning point to perceive clearly where the reform discussion might lead. It did become apparent quite soon that the concept of a 'market-oriented, planned economy' was moribund. It was quickly replaced by the conception of a 'socially and ecologically oriented market economy'.[28] In the meantime the refurbished but not terribly alluring communist party (cast for an interim period as the SED/PDS, the *Sozialistische Einheitspartei Deutschlands – Partei des Demokratischen Sozialismus*) announced its full support for the market economy.

Klaus Steinitz of the GDR Academy of Sciences, Director of a newly founded Commission for Economic, Agriculture, and Social Policy of the SED/PDS, took a position against unemployment and called for a social security net to ease the economic transition for disadvantaged groups. If necessary, he suggested, one should even strive to enter into a social alliance with the Federal Republic.[29]

The combines and enterprises wanted to enjoy some space for

---

27 See 'Marktwirtschaft, Unternehmen und der volkswirtschaftliche Rahmen', *Neues Deutschland*, 13, 14 January 1990, p. 5.
28 Cf. 'Leipziger Thesen zum Wirtschaftsprogramm', (ausgearbeitet vom Bezirkssekretariat und der Kreisorganisation Eilenburg der SED/PDS), *Neues Deutschland*, 22 December 1989, p. 3.
29 Cf. 'Löst die Markwirtschaft alle Probleme?' (Interview mit Klaus Steinitz), *Neues Deutschland*, 24 January 1990, p. 3.

independent decision making in a regulatory environment of parameters not yet clearly defined. The administrative and regulatory institutions (the three industrial ministries and parts of the planning and balancing bureaucracy) still wished to maintain their regulatory activities. The government felt it essential to consider how best to implement reform measures without introducing avoidable additional weaknesses into economic processes. Minister President Modrow advocated that the break with the command economy, which had helped to produce the critical economic situation, must be radical. But he believed at the same time that 'the cutting of the umbilical cord cannot occur so abruptly that it produces economic chaos'.[30]

In January of 1990, Christa Luft, Minister of Economics, declared before leading economics dignitaries from both East and West Germany that the GDR would successfully make the transition to a market economy; it would prove 'economically efficient, internationally competitive, of democratic construction, responsive to social and ecological challenges, and capable of continual renewal'.[31] She affirmed that the process of creating market economic relationships would require placing special emphasis on a reform of property relations, a price reform, steps toward currency convertibility, and measures addressed to the fundamental restructuring of production, export, and import activities. She conceded that these objectives required wise action without undue delay, since crisis phenomena were producing considerable pressure; these phenomena included especially the external obligations of the country, the disproportions in the economy, the lack of competitiveness of the GDR in international markets, the questionable social acceptability of some unavoidable market economic steps, and the income and living standard gaps

---

[30] Cf. 'Stabilisierung der Volkwirtschaft und nächste Schritte der Wirtschaftsreform', Arbeitsberatung der Regierung der DDR mit den Generaldirektoren der zentralgeleiteten Kombinate und Aussenhandelsbetriebe sowie den Vorsitzenden der Bezirkswirtschaftsräte und den Bezirksbaudirektoren am 9.12.1989 (Berlin [East]: Verlag Die Wirtschaft, 1989) p. 6.
[31] Cf. Christa Luft (Stellvertretende Vorsitzende des Ministerrates für Wirtschaft), Rede auf einer Beratung führender Vertreter aus Wirtschaft und Politik der Bundesrepublik Deutschland und der Deutschen Demokratischen Republik im Institut für Unternehmensführung (Berlin [Ost]) January 1990.

vis-à-vis the Federal Republic (dramatized by the newly opened borders and high mobility of GDR citizens).[32] The key elements of the stabilization programme were as follows:

1. *Dismantling the Central Supply System.* New productive capacity was to be created and that already extant was to be expanded, partially through imported equipment and through licensing arrangements. Exports of intermediate goods, especially those with low earning capacity, would be abandoned and the production of spare parts expanded. Increasingly, smaller and intermediate-sized supply firms would be allowed.

2. *The Domestic Market.* To improve the supply of consumer goods, the founding of smaller and intermediate-sized enterprises was to be promoted and the quality of products to be enhanced. Another objective was a more effective export-import orientation on the part of managers. The establishment of additional private and co-operative handicrafts and restaurants was to be encouraged. Wages and salaries would be tied much more closely to worker performance.

3. *Money, Finance, and Credit Markets.* Henceforth, five different types of banks were to function in the GDR: savings banks, co-operative banks, the banks for agriculture and food commodities, foreign trade banks and, above all, the former branches of the central bank. These were to become banks for industry, construction, trade, transportation, etc., under new titles and with newly granted independence. Independent pricing authority would gradually be provided to firms as central pricing institutions were dismantled.

4. *Foreign Trade.* To achieve stabilization in the foreign economic sector, the net value gained from all exports would be re-examined in order to eliminate inefficient exports, although all currently extant contracts were to be honoured. One had initially spoken of restructuring the foreign trade monopoly, but the thrust changed

---

[32] Ibid.

to a recommendation for its elimination. Still, foreign trade rights would be approved by the government. Exports should be promoted through tax breaks, depreciation rates, development programmes, and investment support. Externally, joint ventures, foreign investment participation and the pursuit of international credits by East German firms would be supported by the government.

5. *Science and Technology.* State intervention and directives would no longer be a part of innovation policy, which would now be established by firms and scientific institutions independently. As a framework for the state's promotion of science and technology, indirect measures (e.g., tax relief, interest-free or lower-interest, preferential credits, state finance or risk participation) were foreseen. The process of removing scientific institutions from specific combines was to continue, so that tasks applicable to whole industrial branches (even for the small firms) could be researched.

Modrow's initial reform conception contained too much of the old and too little of the new thinking that was essential. It was in many ways not too much more progressive than plan 'perfecting' conceptions before the *Wende*. But the viewpoints of the responsible economists and political personalities continued to evolve under the unceasing pressure produced by demonstrators and emigrants. The GDR search for a system less hostile to innovation had become very earnest after the cataclysm.

The system being sought as the new year, decade, and era (1990) got a good start would clearly include a devolution of decision authority. According to Schirmeister, 'the high degree of interdependence in our economy can bring greater benefit for independent firms of various ownership types, both for small ones as well as for those of somewhat larger size', if they are willing to implement a production and marketing plan 'with high personal risk'.[33] Let us now consider some of the other reform steps needed at that point.

---

[33] 'Wirtschaftsreform ja – aber wie?' *Op. cit.*

IMPORTANT REFORM NEEDS NOT ADDRESSED BY THE INTERIM GOVERNMENT

The Question of Price Reform

Because we addressed earlier some of the requirements that rationalization of the economic system will necessitate, a brief summary of such measures will suffice here. Decentralization and increased risk taking do not occur in the environment of Marxist-Leninist socialism. A chief characteristic of that environment is the administrative system of non-scarcity prices reflective of the interests and goals of central planners. Most basic, therefore, is the need for a price reform to eliminate or at least reduce some of the current severe price distortions.[34]

We do not refer here merely to the imposition of a new set of centrally-determined prices more closely approximating actual production costs. Genuine price reform must transform the economic system into one which *generates* scarcity prices (reflective of actual supply and demand conditions) on a continual basis. To this point, only markets can provide such a system. Without such prices there can be no means of evaluating enterprise performance, providing information for allocation decisions, stimulating rational choices, or motivating economizing behaviour. Short of this, one cannot speak of efficiency. Indeed, one of the lessons of 1989 seems to be that anything less than the establishment of a system that generates scarcity prices cannot guarantee economic viability.

From the outset the problem of subsidized consumer goods looms especially large when price reform is discussed. For the consumer, these subsidies veil real costs, thus distorting myriads of decisions

---

[34] Thus Heinz Warzecha, General Director of the Combine '7th of October', demands: 'We must desist from a policy of creeping and only parially veiled price inflation, especially with certain consumer goods, which, although they are available in *Exquisit–* and *Delikatläden* (special shops with higher prices for generally higher quality goods, the authors), would be in lower or at best middle quality levels in international markets'. He also adds, 'the yearly inflation rate must also be published'. Cf. 'Was machen wir aus dem Leistungsprinzip? Interview mit Dr. Heinz Warzecha', *Berliner Zeitung*, 1 November 1989, p. 3.

which ultimately leave individual citizens poorer. The traditional socialist decision to reduce dramatically the prices of 'necessaries' [35] through the subsidization of their producers is generally rationalized as an element of social policy. All the socialist countries have fear and foreboding when they consider eliminating these subsidies to reduce the inefficiency of price structures. We would surmise that prior to the debacle of 1989 East European leaders were more concerned that the collapse of their power monopoly could come as a result of price increases rather than from withholding democracy. Even democratic reform socialists were generally disinclined to remove the subsidies hastily; it was more acceptable to let this occur in steps of a size that would avert considerable unrest in the populace. As of early 1990 such steps were already foreseen for the GDR.

It will be recalled (as we pointed out earlier) that such measures as the introduction of the special shops with greater quality and higher prices had already begun to accustom the East Germans to higher prices. The East Germans did not believe the socialist propaganda that capitalism is the only producer of inflation, so one had hope that they would prove more tolerant about higher prices that the Soviets. The Honecker regime, however, had little hope for such tolerance before the cataclysm.

At the end of the Honecker era, subsidies had reached a level of M58 billion annually, and it had been commonly recognized by GDR economists that such subsidies would have to be reduced. The reduction could proceed more gradually if coupled with other measures. Otherwise, considerable unrest could develop among the consumers. Cancelling annual subsidies to the tune of M58 billion for the artificial stability of prices, tariffs, and rents must not only be gradual, but also be coupled with measures to enhance the purchasing power of the citizenry. In the case of housing rents, a housing subsidy could be paid directly to low-income families, permitting the remainder to pay at least some substantial portion

---

[35] The specific goods chosen in the GDR are typical of socialist subsidy practice; they include basic foodstuffs, children's clothing, transportation fares, housing rents, and various services.

of the real costs of their housing. East German economists had numerous such ideas, but Honecker's administration lacked the courage even to consider seriously their implementation.

Not only must subsidies be dismantled; it was also important to abandon the taxation of the more costly durable or 'luxury' consumer goods. The reformation of the capital tax (*Produktionsfondsabgabe*) and the tax on the enterprise's aggregate payroll (*Beitrag für gesellschaftliche Fonds*) was no less necessary. All of these factors distorted the cost structures of the production units and needed to be abolished as scarcity pricing was sought.

Along with these distortions, which were the result of the use of pricing for political purposes (as an instrument of income distribution policy), a series of additional price distortions caused a divergence of consumer goods costs and prices. That pertained especially to intermediate goods, but also to construction and investment equipment, the prices of which were tied neither to demand nor to aggregate economic costs. Moreover, in the period directly preceding the *Wende*, substantially higher prices had been permitted for new and 'improved' products than would be justified by any achieved improvement in the characteristics of the relevant commodity.

It was important that reformers at the outset impress upon their constituencies that in all those sectors where prices were to be decontrolled, precisely because of the ubiquitous supply gaps, inflationary price developments of sometimes considerable dimensions were inevitable. This was not true merely for those goods, of course, which had been subsidized so as to preserve the artificially low prices of necessaries. It held in general because of the shortages that prevailed throughout the economy.

It should be noted, however, that higher prices are exactly what was needed to attract resources for the expansion of competitive productive capacities and, where there is competition, for the encouragement of innovation. Low prices caused the shortages, and unless rewards were made accessible to producers and workers, the supplies would not expand. Rising prices would permit wages also to be increased, making it possible for workers to retain their living standards in the short run, and dramatically to improve them as the system began to function properly in the longer term. For those citizens whose incomes were not affected by the rising prices, social policy would have to ensure that the social security net caught those who would be caught in an incomes/prices squeeze.

Banking and Finance

An independent banking system with appropriate credit policies was required to secure efficient investment and production. The creation of an independent bank of issue (created from the National Bank, or *Staatsbank*)[36] was recommended as the first financial reform step to be undertaken by the government. It would bear responsibility for the stability of the country's currency and assure a rate of expansion of the money supply permissive of economic growth. In the transition to reformed prices and pricing processes, the new bank would provide stability measures and prevent the unmanaged creation of new money. The second step in the reform of the financial system would consist of transforming commercial banks into independent credit institutions and basing the financial tasks of enterprises on meaningful economic conditions. Money and credit policies of such a bi-level banking system would have to function independently of the state's fiscal policies. The response to this conception by the extant Ministry of Finance and Prices was that the traditional role of money had to be restored as a measure of value and performance for every economic agent.[37] From a longer-term perspective the monetary and financial policies of the state must be tied to price and income-distribution policies, and these must be oriented to an effective utilization of the regulatory instruments of monetary policy to promote performance, innovation and competitiveness of GDR firms. It was especially important in a market-oriented reform to take advantage of the flexible implements of finance, credit, and taxation policies – currency exchange rates, interest rates, tax rates, depreciation allowances, and so on.

---

[36] Compare this to the ideas in 'Das Wort der Bank: Interview mit Vertretern der Staatsbank der DDR', *Neue Berliner Illustrierte*, no. 50 (1989) pp. 4–5.
[37] W. Siegert, W. Lebig, and F. Mothes, 'Die Rolle von Geld, Finanzen und Preisen in der Wirtschaftsreform', (Diskussionsvorschlag einer Arbeitsgruppe des Ministeriums der Finanzen und Preise) *Neues Deutschland*, 14 December, 1989, pp. 4–5.

Currency Convertibility

The Honecker era's passive interest in convertibility had to give way under the new conditions to the more pressing need, under marketization processes, to strive to achieve the convertibility of its currency, i.e., the free exchange of the GDR mark for western currencies.[38] The price reform discussed above would have represented a first step in this direction. Convertibility would have been achievable, of course, only over the long term as the GDR economy became internationalized. Greater productivity had to be achieved along with the capacity to penetrate demanding world markets, so that adequate currency reserves could have been acquired. After the opening of the borders there was considerably greater pressure to achieve this complex of objectives, thus enabling East Germans to take advantage of their newly-won travel rights. East German enterprises also needed currency as they pursued more expansive international participation. Many were already taking up their own contacts with firms in the Federal Republic, and were showing special interest in management training.[39]

Developing Anti-Trust Policies

The GDR developed some ideas regarding the disposition of the huge combines very soon after the *Wende*. In discussing Modrow's policy declaration, the parliamentary group of the Free German Youth suggested that inefficient combines could be 'restructured' into small and medium sized enterprises.[40] Because many believed the independence of the enterprises alone would not be sufficient to achieve innovative competition, the GDR's Christian-Democratic-Union (CDU) demanded in its published party programme that the combines be dissolved, i.e., that their monopoly position be terminated through the introduction of forced competition. This was especially important for combines which hitherto had not been and at that time still could not be exposed to international competition.

---

[38] Cf. Hans-Joachim Dubrowsky, 'Aspekte der Konvertierbarket', *op. cit.*
[39] See 'DDR-Führungskader sprengen politische ideologische und bürokratische Fesseln', *Handelsblatt*, 5 January 1990, p. K1.
[40] See *Neues Deutschland*, 18/19 November 1989, p. 5.

Given conditions prevailing in the early months of the Modrow government, it seemed sensible to some to retain a number of the GDR's combines. Industrial realignments were inevitable in any case, since the new government retained only three, rather than the former eleven industrial ministries. In mid-December of 1989, seven combines and two regional economic councils were permitted to make the transition to full financial independence.[41] They were granted greater rights than those of the previously discussed 16 experimental combines under Honecker.

International Cooperation

Minister President Modrow was convinced that a necessary condition for the successful transformation of the previous system was the acquisition of increased international co-operation. He indicated that the GDR was interested in various forms of co-operation with capitalist firms. In the GDR, he observed, joint ventures, investment participation, profit repatriation, and pilot projects in environmental protection were no longer 'foreign words'.[42]

It would have been most beneficial for the GDR to provide a solid legal framework for such forms of co-operation and to relinquish unprofitable, inefficient industrial operations, terminating a number of products that could not be marketed domestically or internationally would have to be terminated. Labour freed from such projects could have been employed in western co-operation projects that would generate hard currency.

Statistical Reform

A final change worth mentioning was East German economic record keeping. GDR statistical data had been a sore point with western economists throughout the history of the country. In a reformed, new order, published statistical data would have had to be greatly improved; the statistical system had a large number of gaps to close.

---

[41] Cf. 'In 7 Kombinaten Beispiele zu neuem Wirtschaftssystem', *Neues Deutschland*, 15 December 1989, p. 2.
[42] Modrow, 'Diese Regierung', *op. cit.*

A mere sampling of the inadequacies would include the aggregate income calculations, the insufficiently detailed industrial data, and the data on investments and the capital stock. The previous system's methods and motives needed radical alteration or elimination, since they satisfied neither the informational requirements of the centre, nor those of individual producers. Finally, the international comparability of the data had to be assured; the nineteenth century ideological construction of socialist national income accounts needed to give way to the realities of the twenty-first century.[43]

LONGER-TERM REFORM OBJECTIVES OF THE INTERIM GOVERNMENT

In order to create stronger performance incentives for the smaller enterprises and the possibility of more extensive independent capital formation, many East Germans considered an additional reform of the tax system necessary. As a first step it was felt necessary to unify and reduce the very high tax progressivity, especially for the handicrafts firms. The discriminatory tax treatment of employed marriage partners and the unification of tax rates for workers in the handicrafts and trades would have to be eliminated.

Given the current East European work environment, in enterprises of all ownership forms, in enterprise councils or among trade union representatives, 'co-determination' or some form of worker participation in decision processes was considered an extremely helpful element of reform. The organs of the enterprise council (or trade union) were to be elected by the aggregate of the employed personnel. At the level of the combines, economics and social councils could be formed.

The DG of the Kombinat Nagema suggested that his firm be

---

[43] Some of the more severe shortcomings include the following: socialist national income accounts understate the economy's product by refusing to count services as production; military expenditures have always been concealed in other statistical categories; and production data have been subject to statistical enhancement.

turned into a joint-stock corporation.[44] Stocks could be issued to the firm's workers, who would be free to sell them to domestic or foreign buyers.

In the future, the state would provide only the framework conditions (such as creating the legal foundations) for private commercial activity.[45] It would secure the participation and plurality of the agents responsible for the functioning of the economy as it sought to establish a consensus for economic policy (of agents representing the Central Bank, as well as of the peripheral organs representing the regions, districts, cities, interest groups, management associations, trade unions, etc.). Overall economic policy would then be addressed to the following tasks: policies for growth and stability (including price stability and full employment), structural policy, and environmental and social policies.

Annual reports and analyses of economic research institutes would be published along with the development of long-term conceptions. To implement its policies the government would utilize only indirect steering instruments ranging from government procurement contracts to certain less direct measures of the performance of selected tasks. Such measures would be applied to foreign trade, consumer goods supplies, energy, prices, ecological tasks remaining in state jurisdiction, strategic commodities, and goods and services of importance for social welfare policy.

The working Group for the Preparation of Economic Reform believed that during the transition period it would not be possible to eliminate the annual economic plan completely, although it should only have orientation value and would be constructed from below upward. As material balancing and output targeting were gradually replaced by contractual relations between firms in the system of central supply, central balances would continue to apply only in the energy sector and for selected raw materials. Such balances

---

[44] See *Handelsblatt*, 26 January 1990, p. 8.

[45] See 'Marktwirtschaft, Unternehmen und der volkswirtschaftliche Rahmen' (Überlegungen der Arbeitsgruppe des Ministerrates der DDR zur Vorbereitung einer Wirtschaftsreform) *Neues Deutschland*, 13/14 January 1990, p. 5.

should increasingly play a strictly informational role as the directive function decreased.

Wages and Salaries

Decentralization was the key word here as well;[46] it was foreseen that the state would provide only framework guidelines, within which the ministries and the industrial trade unions would negotiate concrete working conditions and wages. The centre would give orientation information for the wages and bonus funds established by enterprises, and the most significant consideration in labour earnings would become the worker's performance. Otherwise, concrete arrangements would be nogotiated between the enterprise manager and the elected representatives of the workers. It was suggested that differences in income tax rates between workers and other employees should be eliminated.

Property Forms

Public ownership would remain in only a few key sectors (energy, water, raw materials, heavy industry, transportation, information and communications).[47] Considering the market economy rhetoric of the party after Honecker, the nationalized sector it planned to retain was still a heavy one. It was foreseen, at least, that there would be equal prerogatives for enterprises of all forms of ownership. Private property was to be emphasized in entrepreneurial and handicraft initiatives; the elimination of the former upper limit of ten employees was not only suggested, but achieved. The Working Group also recommended the restoration of the 'people's own enterprise' (*Volkseigener Betrieb* or *VEB*), which until 1972 was either of private or half-state-owned status.

It became acceptable that personal property be invested in enterprises. Condominium-type housing and homes with attached properties could be acquired for personal use. A savings programme for housing construction (*Bausparen*)[48] was proposed, and the

---

46 Ibid.
47 Ibid.
48 In this program, private savings for the purpose of housing construction are augmented by bank loans and government subsidies.

acquisition of bonds at fixed interest rates was suggested as a desirable form of wealth accumulation.

For the transition period the Stabilization Programme envisaged the development of instruments for the macroeconomic management of a market allocation system. Likewise, markets and the associated information relationships still had to be developed. One spoke of gradually coming to grips with a system of currency convertibility and of opening the GDR economy to the world market and the international capital market. Finally, one had to prepare to make the transition to negotiated contract prices or market prices.

For some time rather more than sheer lip service had been given to the need to do these things. It was apparent rather soon after the turning point, however, that substantial progress had to be made quickly, or East German citizens would begin to respond to the alternative course of economic salvation ever more frequently proposed by both East and West Germans – reunification.

Early in 1989 Honecker had promised that the Wall might be standing for a hundred years; the wall was gone within the year. Likewise, after the *Wende* the SED categorically refused to place reunification on the political agenda. Yet by February, Minister President Modrow was talking about preparing the two Germanies for an orderly accomplishment of reunification, already seen as 'inevitable'. One of the four planks of Modrow's unification plan was for an economic and currency union with the Federal Republic as a prelude to reunification.[49]

---

[49] Cf. Terence Roth, 'West Germany's Currency Could Become East Germany's, in First Step to Unity', *The Wall Street Journal*, 5 February 1990, p. A11.

5 Opening the Economy to the West: Reform Efforts Preceding Reunification

It is important, of course, not merely to consider the reform discussion and reform program. Real action was called for in the brief Modrow era, and could not be postponed, given the continuing mass emigration that was in progress.

As we have seen, one measure of reform is the degree to which enterprises can function independently. With increasing enterprise independence, especially in the area of finance, the impacts of central direction on production processes are reduced. As of the beginning of 1990, the centre had reduced the number of orientation coefficients in effect to twelve. These were soon reduced to five: goods actually sold, final products for the citizenry, exports, net earnings, and net earnings taxes. So there was, at least, some movement away from the more centralized environment prevailing before the *Wende*.

In this section we wish to consider the actual progress toward reform that occurred in that brief interim, both in terms of the immediate policy measures undertaken and of the legislative enactments adopted by the interim government. After considering legislation designed to affect the domestic economy, joint venture legislation and policy considerations bearing on currency convertibility will be discussed. Since this chapter relates to actual developments (in contrast to the previous chapter's treatment of conceptual discussions preceding such developments), we will also review limited actions taken by the Federal Republic to provide assistance in the restructuring efforts of the GDR. We will conclude by addressing briefly the insufficiencies of all these initiatives designed to open the East German economy to the West, showing why the East

German people ultimately chose to pursue the path of reunification rather than reform.

EARLY ENDEAVOURS TO INITIATE A REFORM PROCESS

Modest Practical Measures

As a first reform step, subsidies for children's clothing and shoes were removed in January 1990. The removal of these price supports implied price increases for the consumer. As compensation for the price increases in these first two commodity groups, however, family subsidies (*Kindergeld*) were increased through a child's first year by M45 per month and from the beginning of the thirteenth year by M65 per month. Other consumer commodity groups were to be removed from subsidization in sequence.[1] The GDR populace, however, saw these price increases as a very negative development, having been trained under socialism that price stability is an inherent human right. This reaction was probably the reason for the Modrow government's discontinuation of these unpopular measures.

Increases in the rents of dwelling units were also under discussion in the first days of the reform era, but the discussion was soon dropped, leaving this problem to be solved in the future. At that point, the party presidium insisted that priority price increases (subsidy reductions) should be attached above all to those goods which could be purchased by non-GDR citizens and taken away across the open borders. [2]

Heinrich Seickert[3] of the GDR Academy of Sciences contended that the prices of those goods which had no cost elements dedicated for social purposes (education, health, day care, etc.) should be

---

[1] Prices were not increased across the board. Some were actually reduced; these included prices for textiles in winter-end sales, for cassette recorders and accessories, and for ladies hosiery.

[2] Cf. *Neues Deutschland*, 20, 21 January 1990, p. 3.

[3] Cf. Heinrich Seickert, 'Sozialer und ökonomischer Rahmen für den Zwang der Marktwirtschaft', *Neues Deutschland*, 6 January 1990, p. 5

decontrolled.[4] Once the levy component for these purposes was eliminated from production costs (all the way from the raw materials level to that of the final product) the lower prices would render many products price competitive in foreign trade, substantially improving the DM/M exchange relationship. Then GDR production could benefit from the importation of investment goods without being burdened by an unfavourable exchange rate.

Interim Government Legislation for the Domestic Economy

The reform government's conceptions begged to be incorporated as quickly as possible into legislative enactments. These reflected the reform discussions and programmes referred to in Chapter 4.

It was apparent from the outset that the tenure of the Modrow government would be brief. This and other critical factors influenced the sense of urgency to reform: the political influence of the developing opposition parties was powerful; the public interest in all serious reform proposals was strong; the citizenry monitoring proposed change had very high expectations. In this hectic political climate it was possible only with great effort and in the last phase of Modrow's administration to transform incompletely developed reform conceptions into concrete legislation.

As a result, such important laws as the Legislation on Trades (*Gewerbegesetz*),[5] the Law on Founding Private Firms,[6] the Law on the Further Founding and Transforming of Production Co-operatives

---

[4] In socialist economies prices were intended to cover production costs and yield a 'surplus value' kind of return over and above that. These did not constitute profits, as in western economies, but were then used by the enterprise for the well-being of the workers, e.g., for worker housing, day care for workers' children, etc. Sometimes these are funded directly by an enterprise through retained earnings, sometimes they are funded by the centre through enterprise levies into the state budget.

[5] See 'Gewerbegesetz der DDR' (and the associated implementation order, which regulates in particular which trades must be licensed), *Gesetzblatt der DDR*, Teil I, Nr. 17/1990, pp. 138ff and pp. 140, 141, and Nr. 18/1990, p. 169.

[6] Cf. 'Gesetz ueber die Gründung und Tätigkeit privater Unternehmen und über Unternehmensbeteiligungen', as well as the implementation order, *Gesetzblatt der DDR*, Teil I, Nr. 17, 1990, pp. 141ff and pp. 144ff.

in the Handicraft Industries,[7] and the Laws on Agriculture[8] were not enacted until the first week of March 1990. Passage of these laws came on the eve of the first free parliamentary elections held on 18 March 1990. The introduction of free trades and the specification of licensed trades (e.g., real estate agencies, assessors, gambling casinos, art and antique shops, restaurants, etc.), the welcoming of private initiative in the founding or private firms (as members of a chamber of commerce),[9] and finally, the promotion of the handicrafts (joined in a chamber of handicrafts), were important milestones on the pathway toward a market economy. A highly interesting part of reform legislation was that enterprises, both their buildings and equipment, were made available for purchase by private agents; buildings previously under public ownership were to be used for commercial purposes; and the sale of publicly-owned single and two-family homes became subject to the Law on the Sale of Publicly-Owned Buildings.[10]

In order to reduce the heavy tax burden on handicraft firms, members of co-operatives, and other private producers, tax reductions were enacted as early as the end of January, 1990.[11] Relief came for income, corporate, and property taxes on 6 March 1990, at which time some of the system's previous injustices were removed from the tax code. For workers generally, however, only marginal tax changes were foreseen.

---

[7] Cf. 'Verordnung über die Gründung, Tätigkeit, und Umwandlung von Produktionsgenossenschaften des Handwerks', *Gesetzblatt der DDR*, Teil I, Nr. 18/1990, pp. 164ff.

[8] See the 'Gesetz zur Änderung und Ergänzung des Gesetzes Über die landwirtschaftlichen Produktionsgenossenschaften', 'Gesetze über die Rechte der Eigentümer von Grundstücken aus der Bodenreform', 'Gesetz über die Übertragung volkseigener landwirtschaftlicher Nutzflächen in das Eigentum der LPG', 'Gesetz über die unterstützung von Genossenschaften der Landwirtschaft, die durch staatliche Reglementierung mit hohen Krediten belastet sind', *Gesetzblatt der DDR*. Teil I Nr. 17/1990, pp. 133–5.

[9] Verordnung über die Industrie- und Handelskammer der DDR', *Gesetzblatt der DDR*, Teil I, Nr. 15/1990, pp. 112ff.

[10] See 'Gesetz über den Verkauf volkseigener Gebäude' and the Implementation Order in *Gesetzblatt der DDR*, Teil I, Nr. 18/1990, pp. 157, 158.

[11] Cf. 'Anordnung über steuerliche Maßnahmen für Mitglieder von Produktionsgenossenschaften des Handwerks, private Handwerker und Gewerbetreibende', *Gesetzblatt der DDR*, Teil I, Nr. 5/1990, pp. 27f.

Along with the plethora of desperately needed improvements in earlier legislation and regulations, it was appropriate that some first steps were taken toward the conversion of publicly-owned production units to private, corporate forms.[12] An official trustee commission was established to administrate the disposition of public assets,[13] since it was left for the new government to implement any privatization strategy. Unfortunately, practicable instructions were not provided as to how this should be undertaken.

In light of the fears of mass unemployment among the citizenry, which is unavoidable in the process of conversion to a market economy, it was necessary to construct precise regulations on unemployment compensation.[14] Basically, this amounted to M500 per month from the Labour Office for the unemployed; for those earning less than this sum, compensation was to match the previous average net income. In connection with this arrangement was an attempt to retool the unemployed through the provision of an appropriate menu of retraining programmes. In this effort, support was provided not only for the individuals involved, but for the training institutions as well.[15]

Of great importance was the creation of an independent central bank. It was authorized to approve the founding of commercial banks in a two-tiered banking system[16] and to provide them with appropriate supervision. Previously, regulations had provided for

---

[12] See 'Verordnung zur Umwandlung von volkseigenen Kombinaten, Betrieben und Einrichtungen in Kapitalgesellschaften', *Gesetzblatt der DDR*, Teil I, Nr. 14, 1990, pp. 107f.

[13] Cf. 'Beschluß zur Gründung der Anstalt zur treuhänderischen Verwaltung des Volkseigentums (Treuhandanstalt)', *Gesetzblatt der DDR*, Teil I, Nr. 14/1990, p. 107.

[14] Cf. 'Verordnung über die Gewährung staatlicher Unterstützung und betrieblicher Ausgleichszahlung an Bürger wärend der Zeit der Arbeitsvermittlung', *Gesetzblatt der DDR*, Teil I, Nr. 7/1990, pp. 41ff. See also the two implementation orders in Ibid., Teil I, Nr. 12/1990, pp. 93,93.

[15] Cf. 'Verordnung über die Umschulung von Bürgern zur Sicherung einer Berufstätigkeit', *Gesetzblatt der DDR*, Teil I, Nr. 11/1990, pp. 83ff.

[16] See the 'Gesetz zur Änderung des Gesetzes über die Staatsbank der DDR', *Gesetzblatt der DDR*, Teil I, Nr. 16/1990, pp. 125ff.

the continuation of relatively low interest rates, and for the linking of bank credits to appropriate collateral.[17] A first step toward strengthening the municipalities of the republic was that they were empowered to undertake their own credit financing independent of the centre.[18] It was apparent from the beginning that these rather modest legislative reform measures could scarcely begin to create a complete regulatory environment for monetary and credit policy (as is done, for instance, by the Federal Banking Law of West Germany).

Not long after the passage of all this legislation it became apparent that it would soon become redundant. The replacement of East German legal codes by those of the Federal Republic would become just one implication of the process of reunification. Nevertheless, as this brief legislative review hopes to demonstrate, the interim government was determined to move forward with reform. Although these measures were destined to be largely ignored, they would in fact apply during the period directly prior to reunification.

The measures embraced were modest from the perspective of the social market economic system that would soon absorb the former German Democratic Republic. But from the standpoint of the former party under Honecker, they were bold and sweeping.

LEGISLATION ON JOINT VENTURES

As is widely known, the productivity differential between GDR enterprises and West German firms was large. In some sectors, of course, East German productivity was much more than 50 per cent below the West German counterpart (e.g., in energy and metallurgy, in foodstuffs and construction materials). Immediate co-operation between East and West German (or other western) enterprises was necessary to reduce the gap. It was generally believed that the

---

[17] Cf. 'Vierte Verordnung über die Kreditgewährung und die Bankkontrolle der sozialistsichen Wirtschaft', *Gesetzblatt der DDR*, Teil I Nr. 15, p. 114.
[18] See 'Anordnung über die Kreditgewährung an kommunale Einrichtungen', *Gesetzblatt der DDR*, Teil I, Nr. 6/1990, pp. 35ff.

restructuring of production to achieve more efficient forms (while abandoning inefficient operations), could best be achieved through joint ventures.

Unfortunately, the GDR law on joint ventures, which appeared at the end of January 1990, was not bold enough to meet this challenge.[19] A fundamental inadequacy in the law was the stricture that western partners could have a maximum of 49 per cent ownership (minimum of 20 per cent), unless a greater level of western participation were in the express economic interests of the GDR or the enterprise concerned were one of strictly limited size. Permission to establish a joint venture was to be withheld if any danger of control of the venture through a western partner was perceived, or if it was feared that a whole branch might fall into western hands. East German resources could be utilized only by participating GDR firms, and Western partners could participate financially only with western currencies.

When joint ventures were approved, they had to be registered[20] and were subject to the imposition of East German levies. With sales greater than M20 billion or with anticipated average employment of more than 200 workers, approval had to be given by the Economic Committee of the Ministerial Council of the GDR after submission of the required application papers and the provision of economic-technical data on the managerial strategy. In the case of small joint ventures, the regional organs had jurisdiction.[21]

Year-end accounting balances were to be established in terms of East German marks.[22] As had been the practice for GDR enterprises,

----

[19] Cf. 'Verordnung über die Gründung und Tätigkeit von Unternehmen mit ausländischer Beteiligung in der DDR', *Gesetzblatt der DDR*, 25 January 1990, Teil I, Nr. 4/1990, pp. 16–19.

[20] See 'Anordnung über die Führung des Registers der Unternehmen mit ausländer Beteiligung in der DDR', *Gesetzblatt der DDR*, Teil 1, Nr. 6/1990, pp. 34, 35.

[21] Cf. 'Erste Durchführungsbestimmung zur Verordnung über die Gründung und Tätigkeit von Unternehmen mit ausländischer Beteiligung in der DDR', *Gesetzblatt der DDR*, Teil I, Nr. 11/1990, pp. 85, 86.

[22] See Cf. 'Dritte Durchführungsbestimmung zur Verordnung über die Gründung und Tätigkeit von Unternehmen mit ausländischer Beteiligung in der DDR', *Gesetzblatt der DDR*, Teil I, Nr. 11/1990, pp. 88, 89.

a 70 per cent wage tax (*Beitrag fuer gesellschaftliche Fonds*) applied; this drastically reduced the advantage of low wage costs in the GDR.

In the domestic East German market, joint ventures were permitted to negotiate free prices with contract partners, so long as no pre-existing fixed and maximum prices were applicable.[23] Tax regulations for joint production were regarded as inadequate, since they were extremely high as compared to those of other countries. Regulations on the use of hard currencies were also overly restrictive; they mandated that a specified portion of currency earnings be offered to the state for purchase.

A joint venture firm could accept credit in western currencies from either GDR or foreign banks, but the exchange of such currencies for GDR marks had to occur at rates specified by the GDR. The firm was not permitted to open an account with a foreign bank without approval of the GDR's central bank. Generally, public corporations could enter into export agreements independently in the context of GDR import and export regulations. The permissible profit levels and foreign currency transactions could be freely repatriated by Western partners. Should the joint venture be discontinued, a western partner could repatriate only that portion of its profit share which was available in foreign currency at the point of liquidation.

Joint ventures are permitted to extract minerals, although doing so requires application to and approval by state authority. Moreover, mineral extraction is subject to taxation (at a rate of 10 per cent, for example, for lignite, 8 per cent for clay, 5 per cent for salt, 2 per cent of market value for tin, and so on).[24] It was also declared that joint-venture firms would be required to pay 'product-related levies'

---

[23] In a special regulation there is a list of commodity groups with fixed or maximum prices. See 'Zweite Durchführungsbestimmung zur Verordnung über die Gründung und Tätigkeit von Unternehmen mit ausländischer Beteiligung in der DDR', *Gesetzblatt der DDR*, Teil I, Nr. 11/1990, pp. 87, 88.

[24] Cf. 'Vierte Durchführungsbestimmung zur Verordnung über die Gründung und Tätigkeit von Unternehmen mit ausländischen Beteiligung in der DDR – Berechtigung zur Gewinnung mineralischer Rohstoffe, *Gesetzblatt der DDR*, Teil I, Nr. 21/1990, pp. 199ff.

(*produktgebundene Abgaben*) for a large number of products (e.g., M1.10 per litre of gasoline, 75 per cent of the wholesale price of cigarettes, 60 per cent of the wholesale price of table salt, 40 per cent for alcoholic beverages, 25 per cent for beer, 10 per cent for coffee, 20 per cent for coloured TV sets, refrigerators, automatic washing machines, furniture, and cosmetics).[25] The joint venture law was uniformly criticized as inadequate in West German economics circles. The Federation of German Industry had expected a clear and unambiguous (rather than imprecisely formulated) legal foundation for joint ventures, as well as a stimulus for foreign investment. 'Neither premise, calculability or incentive compatibility' was achieved by the regulations of 25 January 1990 pertaining to the founding and functioning of joint ventures.[26] The Working Group of Independent Entrepreneurs also expressed the view that the regulations did not provide a foundation encouraging West German investors to found or participate in a GDR joint venture firm.[27] The legislation and these responses made it apparent that the desperately needed flow of capital into the East German economy would be confined for the time being to narrow parameters.

THE PROBLEM OF CONVERTIBILITY

Reform-oriented specialists perceived after the turning point that the internationalization of the GDR economy could be accomplished only through the convertibility of the mark of the GDR. A better division of labour in the CMEA and the achievement of genuine progress in integration and trade within East Europe would require

---

25 See 'Fünfte Durchführungsbestimmung zur Verordnung über die Gründung und Tätigkeit von Unternehmen mit ausländischen Beteiligung in der DDR – Höhe der produktgebundenen Abgabe', *Gesetzblatt der DDR*, Teil I Nr. 21/1990, pp. 191ff.
26 Cf. 'Ein verheerendes Ergebnis erster Analysen der Joint-Venture-Verordnung Großindustrie und Mittelstand sind sich in der Bewertung einig: Die Verordnung ist unbrauchbar', *Handelsblatt*, February 7 1990, p. 6.
27 Ibid.

convertibility between socialist currencies. The same requirement held for CMEA relationships with the West. In the GDR case an additional pressing consideration recommended at least partial convertibility – the new East German tourist traffic flowing into the Federal Republic and soon into other western countries.

Within the CMEA even the gradual achievement of currency convertibility had already revealed itself to be very problematic, especially because of the extraordinarily variable inter-CMEA price structures of the various product groups. This is why there were, for these traded product groups, a considerable number of dramatically divergent foreign exchange coefficients (indices for calculating currency exchange values in terms of the domestic currency for different groups of goods traded). It hardly seems possible to derive a reasonable exchange rate from a set of average, calculated price relationships between two currencies, since this relationship is dependent upon the dynamic (i.e., continually changing) structure of commodity groups.

The convertibility of socialist currencies could not precede the convergence of price-formation methods and social welfare policies in the CMEA countries. The dismantling of the planning mechanisms and the expansion of free markets would be no less necessary. These things could be brought about in part by increasing the decision authority of enterprises and combines operating in a more competitive environment. But that could prove a very difficult task since the different CMEA countries were attempting to adopt differing reform models and those most progressive in adopting market price formation were experiencing considerable inflationary pressure. Moreover, stagnation in international integration was proving to be a considerable constraint on reform efforts.

To achieve convertibility with western currencies the GDR would not only have to create greater export capacity, but also achieve a high quality level of consumer and investment goods. The capacity to acquire considerable currency reserves available for short-term exchange would have to be created. That would require a performance level from which the GDR economy was still far removed.

The GDR's domestic situation at the *Wende* was characterized by suppressed inflation. There was excess demand expressed in queues and in the halting, reluctant performance of suppliers. The volume of savings and cash holdings in 1989 had reached, as observed earlier, M177 billion (an increase of 28 per cent since 1985).[28] If this excess of money were to be pressed into consumer goods markets in an environment without confidence in the GDR mark, the results could be highly destructive. Some help could be provided in this respect by transferring short-term savings into longer-term forms with higher interest yields. Allowing wealth creation from objects of public ownership (e.g., permitting rental units to be purchased as condominium-type housing) would provide considerable incentives for workers and create new long-term savings patterns.

Another (more external) element of the currency discussion was that of a devaluation of the Mark, that is, a currency reform. Since a whole series of GDR products, especially subsidized goods, were very inexpensive for visitors from the West, the East Germans had great fear of a 'sellout' of such goods. Any acquisition of real estate properties or capital goods by individuals or legal agents from the west was immediately prohibited. Nor was the acquisition of these items through 'straw men' acting in behalf of invisible agents possible. Constraints on trade in consumer goods were applied early; the outward stream of consumer goods through tourism was minimized at the national frontiers through strict customs controls.

Not only West Berliners and West Germans were affected by these controls; visitors from third countries and even GDR citizens were not permitted to sell or give away such goods. So long as such controls were in place, the urgency of a devaluation of the Mark, which would dramatically reduce the value of savings in the GDR, was sharply reduced.

The newly won travel freedoms of GDR citizens contributed to a considerably increased supply of GDR Marks in the West in some periods, depressing the exchange rate there drastically. That development alone should have stimulated East German exports to the West, but the continued existence of the Foreign Trade Monopoly and shortages in raw materials and other production factors, as well

---

[28] Cf. 'Zur Lage der Volkswirtschaft der DDR', *Neues Deutschland*, 17 January 1990, p. 3.

as in intermediate product markets, remained strong impediments to such expansion. Besides, the attempt was being made to avoid 'inefficient' exports.

Inefficient exports prohibited the introduction of a price system adequately expressing real scarcities, especially one that tied into the price system of the Federal Republic.[29] If the GDR desired to develop scarcity prices without being coupled to world markets or the West German market, there would have to be a sufficient number of suppliers functioning independently on the market and forced through earnings and losses to adjust. As long as state enterprises dominated, such adjustment was hindered, since losses were borne by the state budget and political reasons were always found to justify this financial dependence. Finally, an autonomous GDR price system would have been endangered by the possibility of monopolistic behaviour on the part of the large combines. For an integration with the West German price system freedom of payments would have been necessary. Therefore, the GDR Mark had to be rendered completely convertible as soon as possible.

This objective was strongly supported by Ingrid Matthaeus-Maier, a representative of the SPD in the West German parliament, who was an early advocate of the creation of a German-German currency federation. Her view that the GDR could achieve convertibility on its own power only over the long term was widely shared.[30] This early support for a currency union was considered to be an important step toward strengthened co-operation of the two German states.

To tie the value of the GDR mark to the DM under the new conditions would require that a given exchange rate for the GDR mark would have to be supported by injections of currencies from the reserves of the West German treasury and with credit instruments guaranteed by the state. GDR currency would probably have to be purchased in massive quantities to keep its value from falling. Such an internationally recognizable currency arrangement would have permitted the GDR to purchase desperately needed imports of

---

[29] See Hans Willgerodt, 'Die Stunde der Ökonomen', *Frankfurter Allgemeine Zeitung*, 6 January 1990, p. 11.
[30] Cf. Ingrid Matthaeus-Maier, 'Signal zum Bleiben', *Die Zeit*, 19 January 1990, p. 23.

investment and consumer goods. A reduction of the differential in economic well-being between the two countries would have made the exchange rate of the GDR Mark more favourable. A clear signal of this sort, which would certainly have demanded a heavy financial contribution from the Federal Republic, would have had the effect of reducing East German emigration.

Without the exchange rate support of the West Germans, the notion that the GDR and the Federal Republic could form a common currency reserve fund made little sense. From such a fund, the GDR would be forced to accept an increasing currency weakness if deficits produced a growing use of the reserves.[31] Adjustment would force the GDR to undergo structural alterations. It was suggested that increasingly large surpluses for the Federal Republic should be avoided by resorting to the Keynes Plan of 1944. After reaching a specified quota, West Germany would be forced to increase imports from the GDR or have a progressive, negative interest rate applied.[32] a conception of such complexity may have been less desirable than a currency federation supported by the central banking authorities. It could have been transformed later into a currency union with the West German DM as the unified currency.

The Vice President of the German Central Bank, Helmut Schlesinger, spoke out against the early formation of a currency union.[33] He expressed the concern that with open borders and unified currency and price levels all would not be made equal.

---

[31] If too many GDR marks were sold and too many DM were purchased, the value of the GDR M would fall. The currency reserves mentioned would then have to be used to purchase GDR M, thus bringing its exchange price back up to the desired level. If market forces tend to keep pushing the currency below that value, basic changes would have to be undertaken to increase the GDR's export capacity and reduce imports, etc.

[32] Cf. Elmar Altvater, 'Ueber die Chancen der DDR-Mark auf den Devisenmaerkten', *Frankfurter Rundschau*, 28 December 1989, p. 16. Such facilitative adjustments from the West German side would, of course, reduce the downward pressure in the value of the GDR M and also the burden of adjustment otherwise required of the GDR.

[33] Cf. 'Mit sofortiger Währungsunion lassen sich die wirklichen Probleme nicht beheben', (Interview), *Handelsblatt*, 24 January 1990, p. 11.

The productive capacity of East German firms would remain only half as large as their western counterparts which would give rise to two distinct dangers. First, the East German enterprises might attempt to pay the same wages as firms in the West. But they could not maintain such payments and the pressure for subsidies would grow quickly. Or, second, the firms might try to avoid West German wage levels, thus facing the possibility of losing their workers.

Schlesinger spoke against an arrangement officially establishing parallel currencies[34] for the two Germanies, i.e., against tying the DM to a firm exchange rate and admitting the GDR mark as a legal means of payment. That could completely crowd out the mark of the GDR. It would be much better to establish an exchange rate of limited convertibility (more in the direction of under- rather than overvaluation), attempting to maintain this rate economically and gradually adjusting to the large productivity differences. One would have to begin with a reform of the price structures, dismantling subsidies; when prices once reached a competitive level monetary policy would have to prevent the development of inflationary processes.

In any case, Christa Luft, the GDR's economics minister announced that the Mark would be convertible in 1992; even for 1990 a partial convertibility was planned.[35]

Such was the state of the discussion shortly after the turning point. At that time, West German experts felt that the Mark might simply be tied to the DM *after* the appropriate price and finance reforms had been effected. At that time, the German Institute of Economic Research in West Berlin was also in favour of a limited convertibility of the GDR Mark supported by West Germany. It expressed the opinion that a monetary union too hastily implemented would generate some difficult problems. Foremost among these would be the loss of an exchange rate policy, which gives policymakers the option of

---

[34] In reality there had long been an exchange rate for the two currencies, but not officially.

[35] See 'Joint-Venture-Betriebe sind in der DDR nun möglich – Varianten für konvertierbare Mark im Gespräch', *Neues Deutschland*, 26 January 1990, p. 1.

keeping up production through increased exports as they permit the value of the currency to fall on international markets. Without this policy option only the wage mechanism can be used as a policy instrument to deal with the large productivity differences between the domestic and foreign (in this case, West German) economies. Inefficient enterprises could be closed without unemployment only through significant wage reductions. The policy alternatives, that is to say, would be confined to the tradeoff between lower wages or higher unemployment,[36] which is precisely what would be observed with currency unification.

It was the deterioration of the East German economic situation thereafter which caused West German politicians to pursue a currency unification immediately. This was seen as a means of avoiding a demographic avalanche and of taking a first symbolic step toward reunification. It was hoped that putting West German currency into the hands of the East German citizenry would give them hope that their seemingly desperate economic situation would in fact improve and that they need not join the flood of emigrants crowding West German housing and labour markets. Even then, Karl Otto Poehl, President of the Federal Republic's Central Bank believed that talk of a currency union, ultimately advocated even by Hans Modrow, was premature. Currency Union should still follow the economic prerequisites.[37]

THE ASSISTANCE OF THE FEDERAL REPUBLIC IN THE MODROW ERA

One might incline to the belief that more generous assistance from the West Germans in the period after the resignation of Honecker would have given the GDR the capacity to achieve more promising economic change early on. That would have encouraged East Germans to remain at home and work for reform. From the beginning,

---

[36] See 'Reform der Wirtschaftsordnung in der DDR und die Aufgaben der Bundesrepublik', *Wochenbericht der DIW*, No. 6 (1990).
[37] Cf. 'West Germany's Currency', *op. cit.*

however, the Federal Republic made it clear that it had no funds available for a socialist government to misuse. Nor was it interested in shoring up a non-democratic regime that could not demonstrate an ability to win back a thoroughly alienated labour force and citizenry. Let us consider now the preliminary financial role that West Germany was prepared to play in the period under review, especially with the objective of giving assistance for GDR citizens and for the formation of new private enterprises.

As of January 1990, a 'foreign currency fund' of three billion DM replaced the previous, widely publicized arrangement by which 100 DM of 'welcome money' (*Begrüßungsgeld*) was paid by the Federal Republic to each GDR visitor. Approximately three fourths of the new fund was contributed by the Federal Republic.[38] Whereas 'welcome money' was supplied gratis to East German citizens, the new funds had to be purchased with GDR currency. An individual could exchange up to DM 200 per year at favourable rates of exchange: the first hundred at parity and the remainder at 5:1, which on average was an exchange rate of one to three.

With this arrangement for 1990 and 1991 it was also stipulated that GDR mark receipts (9 billion per year) would be earmarked for projects of mutual interest for the two German governments. These included mostly transportation (including border transit) and reconstruction projects for specific cities, especially Brandenburg, Weimar, Stralsund, and Meissen. The objective was to mobilize private initiative to participate in such reconstruction, in other words, to encourage it to follow the signals from the West with its own projects.

After 24 December, West German visitors were no longer required to purchase visas or make the previously mandatory purchase of 25 GDR marks at parity exchange rates. Such visitors could now exchange officially at a rate of 1 DM for 3 GDR marks. A lump

---

[38] It was agreed that FRG payments would be made in the amount of 'welcome money' (1.4 to 1.5 billion DM) plus 750 million DM, and that the GDR would contribute 750 million DM and eliminate the previous minimum exchange requirement for West German visitors, which amounts to a contribution of roughly 1.4 billion DM.

sum payment of 200 million DM, made each year by the Federal Republic to the GDR post office for inner-German telephone service was increased to 300 million DM in 1990. The increased amount was earmarked for the resuscitation of the underdeveloped but also antiquated telephone system.

The European Recovery Program (ERP) special fund was enhanced by two billion DM. Which was to enable the Bank for Reconstruction in Frankfurt to contribute 6 billion DM from 1990–1993 to the support of credit for the GDR's 'middle class'.[39] Two billion DM of this fund was intended for environmental protection and another two billion was earmarked for a general modernization programme for production capacities. An additional 1.3 billion DM was committed to general assistance for newly formed enterprises (*Existenzgründungsprogramm*) and 0.7 billion DM for a tourism programme. Small and intermediate-sized firms were to be favoured. Credits (for a 15–20 year loan, at 6.5 per cent with a five year grace period) were granted in either DM or GDR marks (at an exchange rate of 1DM = M4), but were to be repaid in DM through the newly established Central Bank of the GDR. In inner-German trade the Federal Republic increased its guarantees on deliveries into the GDR from the previous level of 4.5 billion DM to 6 billion.

To promote urgently-needed environmental measures, six air and water projects were arranged between the environmental ministers of the Federal Republic and the GDR. The West Germans committed 300 million DM to supplies deliveries; the GDR promised 465 million marks worth of services and supplies. In November 1989, another eleven environmental installations were negotiated; for these the Federal Republic committed 360 million DM and the GDR M630 million.[40]

To help fund these projects, and to provide for some new assistance, the West German finance minister arranged a special budget

---

[39] Cf. *Handelsblatt*, 18 January 1990, p. 7, and *Frankfurter Allgemeine Zeitung*, 26 January 1990, p. 20.
[40] Cf. *Handelsblatt*, 20 November 1989, p. 12; *Frankfurter Allgemeine Zeitung*, 18 November 1989, p. 4; and *Süddeutsche Seitung*, 28 November 1989.

of net 6.9 billion DM.[41] Supplemental expenditures included 2.15 billion DM for the subsidies to East German visitors, 400 million DM as a first installment for the ERP special fund, 200 million DM for restoration of highways and freeways in areas near the inner-German borders and for railroad-bed reconstruction, new train cars, and locomotives. 90 million DM were committed for information and school programmes, as well as for research and technology transfer. Environmental projects were funded at the level of 140 million DM, and another 75 million DM were made available for medical assistance for GDR visitors. For immediate medical assistance to areas in the GDR left by the exodus of medical personnel without adequate medical care, the supplementary budget allocated 320 million DM. 500 million DM were provided for the temporary lodgings of new immigrants, and 400 million DM were earmarked for West Berlin, which had borne special burdens as a result of recent heavy immigration. A final 2 billion DM were allocated for immediate assistance required by current developments in the GDR or by temporary migratory movements.

These programmes could not be too modest, given the heavy tasks that they had to help perform. Moreover, with further progress in democratization, the hastening transition of the GDR to a functioning market economy, and the need to provide increasing support for individual initiative, it was anticipated that further assistance programmes would prove necessary.

It is apparent when one considers the response of caretaker governments immediately after November 1989, that East German leadership was not yet inclined to embark on a course of genuine economic reform. Even the measures taken allegedly to encourage interaction with the Federal Republic were cautious and restrictive. To a certain extent, this stance may have been a result of an uncertainty as to how to proceed. But it was more likely a reflection of the socialist inclination to cling to the old values and the old ways.

The East German citizenry participated in regular demonstrations in order to keep pressure on Modrow's 'reform' government; these

---

[41] Cf. *Frankfurter Allgemeine Zeitung*, 7 February 1990, p. 1, and *Handelsblatt*, 7 February 1990, p. 1.

efforts continued because the socialists were apparently bent on avoiding substantive economic and social change. The West German government also kept pressure for change on the 'reforming' SED, which, before the elections, continued by default to run the GDR.

THE INSUFFICIENCIES AND INCOMPLETENESS OF GDR REFORM MEASURES

In evaluating the reform efforts of the Modrow government, one should note that its rather short tenure and the unusual circumstances then prevailing did not permit the development and implementation of a well-considered, comprehensive reform programme. The newly formed political groupings, the decision to move forward the date of the first free elections from June to March, the behind-the-scenes struggle with political forces that were bound to old notions, and the simultaneous pressure for speed in the face of continuing emigration all made it difficult to develop well-balanced reform concepts.

It will provide perspective to list briefly some of the very important areas where no (at least no visible) reform measures were undertaken, or where only very imperfect measures were introduced. These include:

1. Reform of the price system and elimination of the distortions incurred through price subsidy programmes. In numerous branches no real decontrol of prices was intended.
2. Reform of the tax and producer levies system. The principal revenue source of GDR socialism was the taxation of products, wages, and earnings of the production units. These needed to be eliminated and normal forms of direct and indirect taxation introduced for compatibility with market institutions.
3. Creation of a differentiated and performance-oriented wages structure.
4. Restructuring and dismantling of combines.
5. Creation of mechanisms to create competitive conditions, including anti-trust legislation and institutions.
6. The dismantling and at least partial privatization of the publicly-owned assets of production units.

7. The privatization of real estate and housing to the benefit of the citizenry (including the appropriate valuation of such properties).
8. Creation of a capital market.
9. Improvement of joint-venture laws, especially regarding the creation of better conditions for foreign investment.
10. The opening of the economy and participation in the division of labour in world markets.
11. The complete elimination of the foreign trade monopoly.

Of course one should not lose sight of the fact that the rapid transformation from a planned to a market economy produces considerable disruption and numerous adjustment problems that are extremely difficult both to foresee and to resolve. Typically, one would expect these problems to be on the agenda of a reforming socialist economy for at least a decade or two, especially since few of the countries involved have developed a public willingness to confront the adjustment problems head-on and without considerable procrastination. For too many decades the peoples of the socialist world were indoctrinated with the notion that the agonies of economic reality were only inherent to the harsh and insecure capitalist order. Therefore, what seemed like bold measures to socialists beyond the *Wende* failed to address basic problems adequately.

CONCLUDING OBSERVATIONS

From the perspective of the market economy, the Modrow government did not introduce a programme of breathtaking reforms. From the perspective of a traditional, socialist society (such as that of the Honecker era), the reform effort was significant. Regardless of the perception, actual reform progress achieved in the Modrow era was a reflection of the will and determination of the newly enfranchised public.

The inevitability of reunification with West Germany became apparent quite early after the turning point. Initially, many East Germans wanted little to do with the notion; after all they had been able to avoid the criminality, drugs, pornography, AIDS, and other such phenomena that troubled their capitalist neighbours. Actually, their freedom from the effects of vice markets was more directly due to the fact that authoritarian East Germany had been a closed society, rather than because it had been of socialist persuasion.

There were those, of course, who would think 'Ah, but the greater humanity and less materialistic characteristics of socialism are exactly the point of the system'. At the turning point many were looking forward to observing to what extent the East Germans, trained for so long in socialist 'values', would retain some of the characteristics that made East German socialism appealing to its adherents. A less stressed society that seemed capable of other than purely material interests could, in fact, be sincerely missed as it disappeared from the world scene. But the greater political and commercial liberties won in the counter-revolution seem much more significant in the long run. Individuals in a commercial society *can* avoid materialism if they choose to do so. But dictatorial societies preferring other than material values simply *do not* provide commercial, political, or spiritual liberties for their peoples. For those newly regained gifts, most of us in the West rejoiced with the East Europeans.

As it turned out, the positive economic aspects of West German society dominated the perception of the economically floundering GDR, and these made some form of federation or confederation more appealing. It was surprising how quickly the East Germans perceived that a radical departure from the old economic order would be necessary to achieve West German economic efficiency. The surviving planning and academic establishments from the *ancien régime* were unable to present convincing argumentation that the planned way was the more secure way. The citizenry perceived clearly and quickly that being the best economy in the socialist bloc was not the same as being on an economic par with the Federal Republic. Moreover, as time passed beyond the turning point, it became increasingly apparent that the performance of the socialist economy had been significantly worse than officially portrayed.

The election of 18 March, which led to a right-of-centre coalition led by the East German CDU, the counterpart of Chancellor Kohl's party in the Federal Republic, was a vote for reunification with the West's social market economy. It is therefore appropriate to consider the process of economic renewal from a Western, market perspective. From that vantage point it seems apparent that it would have taken a reforming GDR a very long time to achieve an economic transformation. Through that period, considerable inflation would have been unavoidable and hidden unemployment would have been exchanged for an expended period of very open unemployment.

The reunification option was not available, or course, immediately after the *Wende*. Early in the transitional period, therefore, a new economic regime had to feel the necessity of unequivocal movement to a course of genuine reform. The future would obviously require market-like competence from the GDR's human resources; immediate economic necessity required greater efficiency and dynamism for the GDR economy.

But even if more extensive measures had actually been inaugurated in the Modrow era, inflation and unemployment would have kept emigration at intolerable levels, vitiating any conceivable reform programme. The underlying social force in all of these developments was the deep economic crisis of Marxist-Leninist socialism in East Europe. As is well known, that general crisis was the direct result of deteriorating economic conditions in the Soviet Union, which ultimately resulted in the liberation of East Europe. In the course of this process, the East German economic crisis became apparent through the peaceful revolution of 1989 and the prolonged, massive exodus of labour. The associated currency convertibility problem and the productivity gap could not have been overcome in the near future by any known or imaginable socialist reform course. Nor would success have been conceivable without extensive economic assistance from the west. As a result, in inner-German relations the offensive shifted to West Germany. By the time the first free elections were due, the economic crisis had become so deep that the GDR was driven into the outstretched economic arms of the Federal Republic.

The discussion of a possible currency reunion suddenly became more than an academic discussion when Chancellor Kohl's government saw the necessity of some dramatic signal addressed to the GDR citizenry. It was believed to be imperative to give the East Germans hope for their economic future, so that they would be willing to remain at home. The wave of emigrants seemed to continue indefinitely. It was also necessary to demonstrate that the Federal Republic was very serious about reunification. What could make this more clear than rapid movement toward monetary union?

Although fraught with some obvious problems, monetary and financial unification have the advantage of eliminating the GDR's very difficult problem of currency convertibility and the prospects of severe inflation for an independent East Germany engaged in economic reform. Price movements will henceforth be constrained, of course, to West German parameters. This inflation problem is not to be underestimated, as we observe from the case of other socialist countries, whose reform endeavours have often halted before the spectre of inflation and its concomitant potential for social disorder.

An additional advantage of monetary union was that the GDR second or shadow economy would largely be replaced by the bright light of an open and free economy. In the process, GDR agents and enterprises were to be thrown into free market waters and be forced to learn very quickly to swim. But at the same time, the less capable would be thrown the very buoyant life jacket of West German social insurance and welfare policies. Any East Germans reluctant to relinquish the social programmes previously enjoyed had to be pleased to discover even more extensive and higher quality programmes available to citizens of the Federal Republic.[42]

The disadvantage of economic unification was the anticipated, extensive unemployment. Because it was impossible to foresee all the transition problems in an experience without precedence in history, one could foretell neither the extent of the unemployment problem nor the reactions of those affected. The populace was understandably nervous and concerned as they moved toward currency union. Many could not be certain their jobs were secure; others were very certain that their jobs were not. But a transformation of economic structures was unavoidable: the decline of socialism was basically due to the misuse of economic resources. The hoarding, squandering, and inefficient use of labour were important manifestations of the general resource problem, and no economic recuperation was imaginable without the elimination of this resource abuse. Hence, unemployment was unavoidable. It should have been some consolation, however,

---

[42] See Phillip J. Bryson, *The Consumer Under Socialist Planning: The East German Case*, (New York: Praeger, 1984), which compares these programmes for the two German states. See especially chapter 8 on social consumption.

that this unemployment was bound to prove of smaller magnitude that the disguised (unproductive) unemployment of the central planning era plus the open unemployment of the economic reform process that would have been necessitated in the absence of reunification.

Fortunately, many new jobs were about to be created. These would be in the underdeveloped services sector, in the establishment of private firms in all sectors, and in the expansion of certain sectors such as construction, machine tools, automotive vehicles, and consumer goods. It could be hoped that the period of extensive unemployment would prove to be relatively brief. Just before monetary reunification, many East Germans expressed optimism that the difficult conditions expected would be overcome quickly. It was often noted that the conditions for recovery were probably better than those prevailing in West Germany just prior to 1948 and the economic recovery later thought of as an 'economic miracle'.

We traced in an earlier section of this chapter the early legislative initiatives of the interim government. Economic reconstruction is no longer a question of the development of GDR laws and policies, since with reunification the question was how the legal system of the Federal Republic could most quickly and effectively be transplanted to the GDR. Some consideration for exceptional and unique problems in the economic development of the East German region was essential. Likewise, it was very important to develop special programmes to promote new firms and sectors and to prevent social disadvantage. Under conditions of reduced GDR independence (the federalist structure of the Federal Republic will still be permissive of a significant degree of cultural and social independence) and a rapid merger of the two economies, the Federal Republic is now prepared to make substantial financial contributions to the economic reconstruction of East Germany, as is evident from the State Treaty (*Staatsvertrag*) of May 1990.

These complex changes call for an analysis of the economics of union between two unequally developed regions. Such an analysis must begin not from the perspective of the centrally planned economy, as was appropriate for this chronicle; it will proceed instead from the perspective of a market economy. The planned economy is already history.

Index